HAND *of* PROVIDENCE

THE STRONG AND QUIET FAITH *of* RONALD REAGAN

MARY BETH BROWN

THOMAS NELSON
Since 1798

NASHVILLE   DALLAS   MEXICO CITY   RIO DE JANEIRO   BEIJING

Published in Nashville, Tennessee, by Thomas Nelson. Thomas Nelson is a trademark of Thomas Nelson, Inc.

Thomas Nelson, Inc. titles may be purchased in bulk for educational, business, fund-raising, or sales promotional use. For information, please e-mail SpecialMarkets@ThomasNelson.com.

Scripture quotations are from THE NEW KING JAMES VERSION. Copyright © 1979, 1980, 1982, Thomas Nelson, Inc., Publishers.

Quotations from MY TURN by Nancy Reagan, copyright © 1990 by Nancy Reagan. Used by permission of Random House, Inc.

Quotations from AN AMERICAN LIFE by Ronald Reagan, copyright © 1990 by Ronald W. Reagan. Reprinted with the permission of Simon & Schuster, Adult Publishing Group.

Library of Congress Cataloging-in-Publication Data

Brown, Mary Beth.
    Hand of providence : the strong and quiet faith of Ronald Reagan / Mary Beth Brown.
      p. cm.
    ISBN 978-1-59555-012-5 (tradepaper)
    ISBN 978-0-78526-053-0 (hardcover)
1. Reagan, Ronald—Religion. 2. Presidents—United States—Biography.
  I. Title.
  E877.2.B76 2004
  973.927'092--dc22   2003028218

Printed in the United States of America

07 08 09 10 11 RRD 8 7 6 5 4 3

This book is dedicated to my husband Floyd;
our sons, Peter and Patrick; and our daughter, Olivia.
I am grateful for their love, prayers, and unwavering faith in me.

CONTENTS

FOREWORD

Hand of Providence is a story of faith. It is an inspiring story of how a seed of faith is planted in the life of a young man by a diligent and caring mother, how that faith blossomed and changed his life, and how, through him, that faith changed America and the entire world. This book highlights my father's deep reliance on the providence of God and the Christian principles by which he lived. Most writers that have written about him fail to recognize the role his faith played in his life. Mary Beth Brown understands how faith can determine our very own destiny.

Growing up as the son of first a governor then a president has not been easy. There are both advantages and disadvantages in being looked at as the "son of" anybody, and, during the time of my father's presidency, my life was filled with many challenges and personal trials. However, the person I could most often turn to in those difficult times was my dad. He had a way of putting everything into perspective, and I believe his determination and perseverance came from his relationship with the Lord.

Dad often shared with me the discussions he had with Billy Graham relaying how much he treasured their time together and how much he admired Graham's work. Even now, with his ever failing health, there is a certain peace that comes from my father, and knowing one day we will be reunited brings me an even greater peace.

Nelle Reagan played an important role in both my sister Maureen's and my life. This book finally brings her out of the shadows of history—how proud my father would be. She was pivotal in developing the Christian values our family has today, and for that we are so grateful. She was always dedicated to helping others and touched the lives of so many.

My father is a godly man. He loves God. When he decided to run for president, he didn't do it to raise himself up, to be admired, or to have others think he was great. He didn't do it out of selfish reasons or because it is the most powerful position in the country. He did it out of duty. He believed God had called him to run for president. He believed God had things for him to do.

I hope this book not only brings you a better understanding of who Ronald Reagan is, but deepens your commitment to the Lord. The greatest gift my father ever gave me was the simple knowledge that I would see him in heaven one day. I pray you are there with us.

—Michael E. Reagan
January 2, 2004

INTRODUCTION

For you see your calling, brethren, that not many
wise according to the flesh, not many mighty, not
many noble are called. But God has chosen the foolish
things of the world to put to shame the wise, and
God has chosen the weak things of the world to
put to shame the things which are mighty . . .

1 Corinthians 1:26–27

President Ronald Wilson Reagan's death on June 5, 2004, brought forth an overwhelming outpouring of emotions from our nation for America's fortieth president. The week of national mourning included hundreds of thousands of Americans passing by his casket to pay their respects, both at the Ronald Reagan Presidential Library in California and at the U.S. Capitol in Washington DC. After his funeral service at the National Cathedral, the week ended with the burial internment at his chosen site. With a blazing sun setting in the sky of his beloved California, America said goodbye. But Reagan chose more than just the site of his burial. He also chose some of the speakers and music for his own funeral. Through his choices, America learned much about her beloved president and what was important to him. It was that week following his death that much of America had a glimpse of his strong and yet quiet religious faith. President Reagan had one more thing he wanted to communicate to Americans—and he did it at his funeral, through music and word.

Many years ago, Reagan asked Sandra Day O'Connor, whom he had appointed to the Supreme Court, to read at his funeral from the 1630 sermon by Pilgrim John Winthrop, which encapsulated his vision for

America. Reagan often described America as being "a shining city on a hill" which is used in this sermon as a reference to Jesus' words in the Bible. The passage which Reagan requested Justice O'Connor quote reads as follows:

> Now the only way to provide for our posterity is to follow the counsel of Micah, to do justly, to love mercy, to walk humbly with our God.
>
> We must delight in each other; make others' conditions our own; rejoice together, mourn together, labor and suffer together, always having before our eyes our commission and community in the work, as members of the same body.
>
> The Lord will be our God, and delight to dwell among us, as his own people.
>
> For we must consider that we shall be as a city upon a hill. The eyes of all people are upon us.
>
> So that if we shall deal falsely with our God in this work we have undertaken, and so cause him to withdraw his present help from us, we shall be made a story and a byword through the world.

While still serving in office with then Vice President George Bush, Reagan asked him to speak at his funeral. We all saw Bush carry out his wishes on that June morning at the National Cathedral. Good friend former prime minister of Great Britain, Margaret Thatcher, who shared Reagan's worldview and had worked with him to bring down the Berlin Wall, also spoke at the funeral (via a taped message), per Reagan's request years earlier. "To Ronnie, 'Well done, thou good and faithful servant.'" Thatcher wrote in a condolence book for her friend and political ally.

During that week of mourning, but also a celebration of his life, close friends and family who knew Ronald Reagan well spoke of his Christian faith and how it was central to his life and made him the man that he was.

Reagan's favorite song, *Battle Hymn of the Republic*, along with other patriotic music and hymns such as *Amazing Grace* and *Just As I Am* were played and sung at the memorial services, just as he had arranged so many years before.

Fifteen years have passed since President Reagan left the White House, but he still is remembered fondly and with admiration as one of America's greatest presidents. The country's eyes were once again focused on this truly great man, but it left many wondering: what was the key to his success, what made him the great man he was, and do what he did? Americans wanted to understand and know as much as they could about Ronald Reagan.

I had found myself asking some of these same questions a few years earlier . . .

On a magnificent day in June 2001, I stood on the lawn of President Reagan's Ranch, Rancho del Cielo, and took in the glorious sunlight surrounded by vast and beautiful scenery. Because of my husband Floyd Brown's position as executive director of Young America's Foundation, the organization that saved this special place from destruction, I have had incredible opportunities to meet interesting individuals closely connected to America's fortieth president.

On this particular June day, I was with Michael and Colleen Reagan. Mike, who is an outspoken Christian and host of his own successful radio show, was regaling my husband and me with stories about his dad. The joy of visiting the ranch had unleashed an outpouring of emotion in Mike, and I listened carefully as he told us a compelling story about the faith of his father. His story struck a chord in me, but I also knew his picture of his father conflicted with much of what I had read about the man in biographies and in the media.

When your husband has responsibility for overseeing the historic preservation of a presidential site, you read everything you can about the man. My husband is a long-time Reagan fan who worked in the 1976 and 1980 campaigns. We were married in 1983 and moved to Washington DC. He had a dream of working for Reagan and soon was a political appointee in his administration. During those years, I attended several events at the

White House, including a Rose Garden ceremony where my husband stood on the stage next to the president. I say all of this to make the point that much of my adult life has been spent observing and hearing stories about President Reagan.

So when the picture Mike was painting on the lawn of Rancho del Cielo was so different from what I had seen from journalists and knowledgeable Reagan scholars, I began to wonder who was right. I became curious. My training as a researcher has always caused me to ask tough questions. Mike inspired me to ask more. As I have learned, it's very important that we have the true facts, not the assumed ones, about Ronald Reagan.

Ronald Reagan is, according to recent opinion polls, the most popular of the modern presidents. He is credited with restoring America's economy after the most difficult economic crisis since the Great Depression. He is also credited with—as former British Prime Minister Margaret Thatcher said—"ending the cold war and tearing down the Berlin Wall without firing a shot."

In 1994, Reagan announced that he was entering the "sunset of his life" as a victim of the life-destroying disease of Alzheimer's. This announcement only strengthened his outstanding reputation and fueled renewed interest in his inspiring and successful life.

Throughout his distinguished career, Ronald Reagan has confounded the elite opinion makers. He won landslide victories as president despite the overwhelming opposition of media pundits, political professionals, and university professors. These individuals who control the pens that write our history freely admit that Ronald Reagan confuses and confounds them.

Edmund Morris, the official biographer of Ronald Reagan, has even been quoted as calling him an "enigma." Morris complains that he doubts anyone can really understand Ronald Reagan. A flurry of recent best-selling books have attempted without success to unravel the puzzle of his life and personality. I would contend they are unable to understand Reagan because of inherent problems with the internal secularist worldviews of the experts and biographers who are attempting to explain him.

Current biographers have looked at Ronald Reagan through jaded eyes. When you see someone through the eyes of a secular humanist, you will fail to see the vibrant Christian faith and fruits of the Holy Spirit that were evident in the life of Ronald Wilson Reagan. To understand Ronald Reagan, his decision-making process as president, and the unprecedented success it produced, you must understand his reliance on God.

The writers who have attempted to explain Ronald Reagan have ignored this most important aspect of his life: his faith in God—who rules in the lives of men and women who are committed to Him. Reagan believed he had a calling upon his life from God, and he wanted to fulfill that calling.

The purpose of this book, then, is to help individuals who are studying Ronald Reagan to learn that his Christian faith was what accounted for his success.

It is amazing to me how consistently his former political associates attest to his deep faith in God. Lyn Nofziger told me that Reagan was "born again." Attorney General Ed Meese, Mike Reagan, Judge William Clark, and John Barletta have all told me about his deep, personal, and strong faith. Yet few of the writers, even the unabashed fans of President Reagan, have ever given his Christian faith an appropriate airing.

The second reason I wrote *Hand of Providence* was that through researching President Reagan's life and words, I found my own faith had increased. I was helped by things Reagan or his mother Nelle had said and by their example of how they handled trials and problems in life. After finding all this wonderful material through my research which had helped me, I wanted to share it with others because I thought it could help them also. Since the book was first published, I have heard from many readers that they too found Ronald Reagan and his mother to be very inspiring, and they have been helped by reading his own words about his faith in God.

So now you know how this project started. I became curious about his faith. The following pages are my humble attempt to tell the story that I felt had not been told before—by even his most honest biographers. In this book, I have attempted to use Ronald Reagan's own words and writings as much as possible. Moreover, I have spent hundreds of hours reading other primary source material, and I have had firsthand interviews with many of Ronald Reagan's staff, friends, and observers.

In studying his life, words, and actions, I discovered that Ronald Reagan is a deeply religious man who cannot be adequately appreciated or explained without understanding his Christian faith. My hope and prayer is that you will read every page with an open mind. Just maybe, if you have never before considered the Christian life, you will do as I know Ronald Reagan did and look to Jesus Christ for the solutions to life's perplexing questions and problems. This is a cause that was near and dear to President Reagan's heart. As he said when asked about his faith, ". . . having accepted Jesus Christ as my Savior, I have God's promise of eternal life in heaven, as well as the abundant life here on earth that he promises to each of us in John 10:10."

Sincerely,
Mary Beth Brown
Santa Barbara, California

HAND *of* PROVIDENCE

I now seem to have her faith that there is a divine plan, and while we may not be able to see the reason for something at the time, things do happen for a reason and for the best. One day what has seemed to be an unbearable blow is revealed as having marked a turning point or a start leading to something worthwhile.

—RONALD REAGAN,
discussing his mother's faith in God

CHAPTER 1

THE HAND OF
PROVIDENCE

*And we know that all things work together for
good to those who love God, to those who are the
called according to His purpose.*

ROMANS 8:28

He leaned back in the luxurious chair reserved for the president of the United States on Air Force One. The two men, fortieth president of the United States, Ronald Wilson Reagan, and his grown son, Michael Edward Reagan, were deep in conversation as their plane sped onward toward Point Magu, California. *One, two, three, four, five, six, seven, eight, nine,* the president sat quietly counting his fingers.

"What are you doing, Dad?" asked Michael. "I'm counting the months until I will be out of office and I'll be able to attend church again," answered the president.

This conversation with his father was relayed to me by Michael

Reagan in June of 2003 during a dinner at the Mimosa French Restaurant not far from the Reagan Ranch in Santa Barbara, California. Michael recounted the story with the passion a man has for an event that has been seared into his memory. I later learned that the trip he took alone with his father on Air Force One was taken shortly before Easter of 1988. Nine months later, in January 1989, Reagan left office after having served two terms as president.

Michael continued, "My father was really looking forward to the time when he was out of office and could attend church again. The reason he had stopped going to church while president was because he didn't want to put other people's lives in danger." Michael said that his dad still remembered all too vividly the people who had been severely injured and almost killed because of the assassination attempt against him. According to Michael, "Dad was willing to stop going to church, something that was very important to him and he liked to do, to prevent risking the lives of other innocent people, if another assassination attempt was made on him." But Michael said he encouraged his father to make an exception this Easter weekend and attend church. President Reagan paused a moment, then smiled, and said, "I think I will."

Early Easter Sunday morning, after he'd eaten a hearty breakfast, Reagan called John Barletta, head of the Secret Service at the Reagan Ranch, to have the helicopter readied for a short trip to church. The president attended a small country church in the Santa Ynez valley near his beloved Rancho del Cielo. This church had been a regular house of worship for him when he was at the ranch before his presidency. Sadly, he was still attacked by the liberal press for not attending church during his presidency, when it was actually something that was truly important to him—and his reason for not going was to protect lives.

This exchange between father and son showed the power and lasting impact of the near-tragic event that had occurred seven years earlier and how this attempted assassination had radically altered President Ronald Reagan's life. Reagan never wanted to put anyone in harm's way again.

SAVED FOR A HIGHER PURPOSE

The president walked out of the side entrance of the Washington Hilton Hotel on a gloomy, gray afternoon in the spring, wearing his new blue pin-striped suit. Smiling and waving with his entourage of aides and Secret Service agents, he was met by a group of onlookers—mostly press photographers, TV cameramen, and reporters corralled behind a red velvet rope. It was March 30, 1981, the seventieth day of his presidency, and Reagan had just given a speech to the Construction Trades Council inside the hotel. The president's schedule was routinely printed in the *Washington Star* newspaper, as it was that day, giving the time and place of his speech. Anyone could find out where the president would be that day simply by looking it up in the daily newspaper, and someone did just that. That person was also waiting in the crowd outside the hotel. His name was John Hinckley Jr.

Because it was a warm and muggy day, President Reagan had not worn his bullet-proof vest. It was an oversight that nearly cost him his life. The president reasoned that his only exposure to the outside would be a short, thirty-foot walk from the hotel corridor to the car, and, besides, the vest restricted the movement of his arms, which he liked to use in gestures as he gave his speech. The president was to speak to a group of 3,500 people, his largest audience since the inauguration in January. He leisurely headed toward his limousine (code named "Stagecoach" by the Secret Service) to return to the White House. Just before reaching the car, his assailant became visible—and the history of our nation and the world was nearly changed forever.

John Hinckley Jr. carried a .22-caliber Rohm snub-nosed revolver under his trench coat. It was loaded with six specially made bullets. He was a man on a mission—fully prepared to kill the president of the United States.

Only after the assassination attempt did we learn that Hinckley had written a letter to Jodie Foster, the young actress with whom he was obsessed. He told her in a letter, "I would abandon this idea of getting

3

Reagan in a second, if I could only win your heart and live out the rest of my life with you. . . . I will admit to you that the reason I'm going ahead with this attempt now is because I just cannot wait any longer to impress you." Hinckley closed the letter saying, "I'm asking you to please look into your heart and at least give me the chance with this historical deed to gain your respect and love."

President Reagan waves to onlookers immediately before being shot by John Hinckley Jr. at the Washington Hilton Hotel, 30 March 1981. (Courtesy of the Ronald Reagan Library)

Hinckley had to have the right opportunity, and this gray, muggy day in March was it. A reporter tried to get the president's attention shouting, "Mr. President!" and "Mr. Reagan!" Hinckley's moment had arrived. He shoved several bystanders out of the way, assumed a crouching position, pulled out his weapon with a professional double-grip, and took aim.

Pop, pop, pop, pop. The bullets sounded like firecrackers, and the acrid smell of sulfur filled the air. Two seconds. That's all it took to change a life . . . and the world.

Down went White House Press Secretary James Brady, who was in the line of fire and hit in the forehead with the first bullet. Brady was left lying facedown in a pool of blood. The second shot went astray, but the third hit Washington patrolman Thomas Delahanty in the back of his neck causing him to fall next to Brady on the ground. With tremendous courage, Secret Service agent Timothy McCarthy used his body as a human shield and took the fourth bullet intended for President Reagan. The bullet hit McCarthy in his lower right rib cage, throwing him backwards three feet onto the sidewalk beside Brady and Delahanty.

By now, Secret Service agents, police, and bystanders had tackled Hinckley, but he was still able to shoot one last bullet before he went down. This fateful bullet hit the limousine and ricocheted through a small gap between the body of the car and the door hinges. The bullet found its target, though, hitting the president's chest under his left arm and making a small hole in his skin as it headed for his heart. Jerry Parr, the head of the Secret Service detail, threw the president into the car, heroically landing on him to shield him from any more gunfire. As Parr shielded him, the president felt an excruciating pain in his chest. Reagan initially thought that one of his ribs had been broken when Parr landed on him.

Parr yelled, "Move out!" to Drew Unrue, the driver of the limousine, and told him to return to the White House. Unrue hit the accelerator and raced toward the president's home. Parr, an experienced Secret Service agent, ran his hands under the president's coat, feeling his sides and chest and running his fingers through the president's hair on the back of his head to check for blood. There was none.

But just when Parr was satisfied that the president had escaped unscathed, Reagan began coughing up pink, frothy blood—obviously, freshly oxygenated blood from the lungs. Agent Parr instantly knew that the president had been seriously injured and told the driver to head for George Washington University Hospital. By now, President Reagan was having great difficulty breathing. I remember learning in nursing school that one of the scariest feelings you can experience is when you're in respiratory distress and you can't get enough air to breathe, no matter how hard you try. You feel like you are suffocating. Time was running out. The limousine driver gunned the engine in a desperate attempt to reach the hospital before it was too late.

The presidential phone in the hospital emergency room rang. This presidential phone was to be used only in an extreme emergency. This was definitely it. The nurse who answered it was told to prepare for the presidential motorcade to arrive for immediate emergency care. The emergency room sprang to life in preparation for its incoming patient.

Mike Deaver, whose presidential control car (a mobile communications center) had pulled up to the hospital just after the president's car arrived, describes what he saw as President Reagan walked into the emergency room: "I saw Reagan get out of the car unaided, look to both sides, and give a tug to his pants. I think he actually buttoned his suit jacket. So far, so good. He walked toward the emergency room doors unassisted, with a pair of agents at his sides, but as soon as he was through the doors, out of public view, the strength in his legs abandoned him."

Reagan collapsed and was lifted onto a stretcher. The nurses quickly pulled off his jacket and cut off his shirt. Dr. Price, an emergency room physician, later recounted what happened in Paul Thomsen's *Operation Rawhide*, "I listened, but there was no sound in his left lung, and his blood pressure was double zero. There was no pulse." The president was hovering near death.

Blood and other fluids were being forced into his system through three IV lines while a drainage tube was pouring blood out of his side. Reagan's systolic blood pressure rose to eighty. Dr. Price rolled the president over and noticed a small slit, like a button-hole, under Reagan's left armpit. The doctor suspected that this was the bullet hole and had the area x-rayed.

President Reagan knew that doctors and nurses were working on him feverishly, fighting to save his life, but he was still having trouble breathing. His skin had turned so pale that Nancy Reagan remembers, "He was the color of paper—just as white as a sheet, with dried blood around his mouth."

Reagan later recalled looking up from the gurney, trying to focus his eyes on the square ceiling tiles, and praying. While he was lying on the gurney, half-conscious, he realized that someone was holding his hand.

"It was a soft, feminine hand," he writes in his autobiography, *An American Life*. "I felt it come up and touch mine and then hold on tight to it. It gave me a wonderful feeling. Even now I find it difficult to explain how reassuring, how wonderful, it felt."

He goes on to say, "It must have been the hand of a nurse kneeling very close to the gurney, but I couldn't see her. I started asking, 'Who's holding my hand? . . . Who's holding my hand?'" When he didn't hear any response, Reagan said, "Does Nancy know about us?"

He continues, "Although I tried afterward to learn who the nurse was, I was never able to find her. I had wanted to tell her how much the touch of her hand had meant to me, but I never was able to do that."

ANGELS WATCHING OVER HIM

Reagan had experienced a similar event when he was critically ill with viral pneumonia many decades before. He had written about this encounter in his earlier autobiography, *Where's The Rest of Me?* At the time, he was working on a movie with Shirley Temple that he admits he was "less than happy about doing," when he became deathly ill. He writes, "But while the studio was sleuthing around the hospital to see if I was really there, my next of kin were being notified that the hospital might be my last address."

"Days and nights went by in a hazy montage in which I alternately shivered with chills or burned with fever," says Reagan. He was lying in bed wrapped up in blankets waiting for the fever to end, but instead his temperature just kept getting higher. He describes his touch-and-go situation in this way, "Finally I decided I'd be more comfortable not breathing. I don't know what time of night it was when I told the nurse I was too tired to breathe. 'Now let it out,' she'd say. 'Come on now, breathe in once more.'"

"This went on, over and over, with her arguing me into another breath when all I wanted was to rest and stop making the effort. Wherever she is and whether she remembers our midnight contest or not, I don't suppose I'll ever know, but the memory is vivid to me. She was so nice and persistent that I let her have her way, and kept breathing out of courtesy. The sweat came and washed me back down the divide I'd been climbing."

Were these mysterious nurses whom Reagan never could find actually angels sent by God to help him survive in his hours of desperate need? Were they there to save him so he could carry out God's plan for his life?

In *Angels Don't Die,* President Reagan's daughter, Patti, recounts seeing her father in the hospital the morning after the assassination attempt in 1981. "He actually didn't look frail; he looked almost ethereal. There was a light in his eyes that made me think, then and still, that he saw something—visited with God, listened to the counsel of an angel—something. My mother has since told me that he woke up at one point after the doctors had operated on him, unable to talk because there was a tube down his throat. He saw figures in white standing around him and scrawled on a piece of paper, 'I'm alive, aren't I?'

"When my mother first told it to me, we discussed how logical it is to assume that the figures in white, standing around my father, were the doctors and nurses who were tending to him. But maybe not, we said; maybe he did see angels. We left it with a question mark. Then I repeated it to a friend—a nurse—who pointed out to me that no one in a recovery room or in intensive care is in white; they're all in green scrubs. I phoned my mother and told her, and her reaction was, 'I didn't even think of that, there was so much that day—but you're right.'"

Michael Reagan, speaking to students at a Young America's Foundation Summer Conference in July, 2003, about the same incident, told the group, "Patti believes they were angels, and so do I."

Stories of the presence and guidance of angels can be powerful. In his classic book, *Angels: God's Secret Agents*, Billy Graham writes many wonderful, comforting things about angels in his book and, after a lifetime of extensive research on the topic, comes to these conclusions: "Both angels and the Holy Spirit are at work in our world to accomplish God's perfect will. God uses angels to work out the destinies of men and nations. He has altered the courses of the busy political and social arena of our society and directed the destinies of men by angelic visitations many times over."

Angels are mentioned in the Bible over three hundred times. According to Scripture, they have helped the children of God in difficult circumstances and are prepared for any emergency. And, when necessary, they can become visible. Graham says, "God uses both men and angels to declare His message to those who have been saved by grace," and has ordered angels to minister to men. As proof, he quotes from the Bible, where in Hebrews 1:14 the writer says: "Are they [angels] not all ministering spirits, sent forth to minister for them who shall be heirs of salvation?"

Angels have faithfully carried the message of God's will in times of oppression, discouragement, and failing endurance. Graham says God's restoring servants, His "heavenly messengers," have encouraged, sustained, and lifted the spirits of many discouraged saints and have changed many hopeless circumstances. Angels have ministered the message, "All is well," to fully satisfy the physical, material, emotional, and spiritual needs of His people.

Billy Graham says the most important characteristic of angels is that they work on our behalf. "They are motivated by an inexhaustible love for God, and are jealous to see that the will of God in Jesus Christ is fulfilled in us."

God assigns angelic powers to watch over us "for we have been made a spectacle to the world, both to angels and to men" (I Corinthians 4:9). Graham notes, "They superintend the events of our lives and protect the interest of the Lord God, always working to promote His plans and to bring about His highest will for us."

After undergoing surgery to remove the bullet that nearly killed him, President Reagan described being surrounded by "people in white." We find in Psalms 34:7 the following promise: "The angel of the Lord encamps all around those who fear Him, and delivers them."

According to Graham, the Scriptures are full of dramatic evidences of the protective care of angels in their earthly service to the people of

God. Graham encourages Christians to be aware of the operation of angelic glory and quotes from Psalms 91:11: "He will give his angels charge of you, to guard you in all your ways."

"Someone was looking out for us that day," President Reagan concludes in his autobiography. Indeed, the Lord was.

PROVIDENCE IN OPERATION

Dr. Benjamin Aaron, the chief of cardio-thoracic surgery at George Washington University Hospital, heard on his office radio about the assassination attempt on President Reagan's life. Almost simultaneously, his beeper went off calling him to the emergency room, and he was then paged on the hospital intercom: "Dr. Aaron to the emergency room. STAT!"

At this point, Dr. Aaron had just worked thirty-three hours with little sleep, starting Sunday with emergency heart surgery and going on to his two scheduled surgeries. Now, it was Monday afternoon, and he was exhausted. He quickly said a prayer before heading to the emergency room, "Lord God Almighty, You'll have to give me strength now—I'm at the end of my rope—this will have to be on Your power!" Emboldened by his faith, Dr. Aaron ran off to receive his critically wounded patient.

After Dr. Price briefed him on Reagan's medical status, an orderly ran up to Dr. Aaron with an x-ray of the president's chest. Dr. Aaron studied the x-ray and saw the bullet was next to or possibly in his heart. At this point, according to Dr. Aaron, President Reagan had lost one-third of his blood supply, had severed several major blood vessels, and had briefly lost his blood pressure and pulse.

Dr. Aaron had to make a quick decision. He told his associates, "In my opinion, we stand a good chance of losing him if the bleeding isn't stopped shortly. The decision is mine and mine alone—we are going to operate." He then spoke to the president: "Mr. President, you've got a bullet in your chest. I think it's best we take you to the operating room, open your chest, get that bullet outta there, and fix up the damage." Reagan responded immediately: "Whatever you think you need to do, I put myself in your hands. I guess we'd better get on with it."

After scrubbing in preparation for surgery, Dr. Aaron entered the operating room filled with his team of nurses and doctors. Several Secret Service agents stood along the back wall of the operating room to protect the president from any other possible threat to his life.

As he began to operate, Dr. Aaron prayed to himself, "Lord, I know You are a sovereign God who controls all events, and it's to You I commit this operation. If it be Your will, O Lord, guide me and heal this man through these hands."

Just before he went under the physician's scalpel, President Reagan broke the tension in the room in a loud, clear voice, "I hope you guys are all Republicans!" and then smiled when Dr. Giordano, a long-time Democrat, replied, "Today, we're all Republicans, Mr. President." The anesthesia was then administered.

Dr. Aaron carefully began the thoracotomy, cutting through Reagan's chest wall. "It took me forty minutes to get through that chest," Dr. Aaron told Nancy Reagan after the surgery, "I have never seen a chest like that on a man his age." When he reached the president's heart, it was beating strongly and was in "extraordinarily good shape." He couldn't see the bullet but surmised from the x-ray that it was resting against the wall of his left lung, less than one-half of an inch away from his pulsating heart. Dr. Aaron began to probe the area with his fingers.

Tension grew in the room as the doctor tried unsuccessfully to find the deadly bullet. Dr. Aaron knew that if he dislodged the bullet into a blood vessel in the lung, it could easily be sucked into the blood stream, then to the heart, and that could cause instant cardiac arrest. Dr. Aaron also faced the possibility that the bullet could pass through the heart and on into the brain, causing instant death for President Reagan.

Unable to find the bullet with his fingers, the doctor tried using a catheter tube and successfully traced the path of the bullet. He found it when the catheter stopped at the end of its path. Slicing through the lung tissue, he was able to make an opening and gently remove the lethal bullet with his fingers. "There it is. Thank God," the doctor said as he lifted up the bullet to show the others in the room. There was a collective sigh of relief when they saw the bullet. A Secret Service agent immediately approached him with a collection cup and motioned for him to place the bullet in the cup. It was sent off to the FBI for ballistics tests.

At the FBI ballistics lab, tests revealed that this bullet—which had rested within an inch of the president's heart—was a specially-designed bullet used for big-game hunting. The bullet was aptly named the "Devastator" because it was made to flatten out and cause maximum damage as it ripped its way through a body. In addition, the tip of the bullet was filled with a chemical called lead azide, which was designed to explode upon secondary contact with something hard—like a bone. As it exploded, it would cause additional damage to a six-inch area of a person's body. The chemical alone is a toxic poison. So dangerous is this kind of bullet that one of them exploded while an FBI ballistics expert was examining an identical bullet in the lab. Thankfully, he was wearing safety goggles and escaped injury. Still, amazingly enough, the bullet did not explode in President Reagan's chest even though Jerry Parr had landed on him in the limousine and Dr. Aaron had probed for it with his fingers.

While recuperating in the recovery room, President Reagan had a tube down his throat, making it difficult to speak, so he communicated by writing notes on a pad of paper. One such note was a reminder of his earlier career as an actor. The note he handed to a nurse read, "I'd like to do that scene again—starting at the hotel." Scribbling on another piece of paper he wrote, "Winston Churchill said there is no more exhilarating feeling than being shot at without result." Gaining momentum, he wrote another humorous note that said, "Send me to L.A. where I can see the air I'm breathing."

Many "miraculous factors," as the president called them, added up to the saving of his life. And if any one of them had occurred differently, he most certainly would have died that day in March 1981. President Reagan points out in his autobiography that most of the doctors who practiced at the hospital had been attending a special meeting that afternoon:

President Reagan walks with Mrs. Reagan inside the George Washington University Hospital four days after the nearly fatal shooting, 3 April 1981. (Courtesy of the Ronald Reagan Library)

"Within a few minutes after I arrived, the room was full of specialists in virtually every medical field." He had turned toward the reporter at just the right time when he was shot; otherwise, the bullet might have hit directly into his heart. Reagan biographer Edward Morris points out that the limousine miraculously reached the hospital, although driving in uncontrolled traffic, in just three-and-a-half minutes. And the bullet didn't explode while Dr. Aaron was exploring for it—or at any other time since it had entered Reagan's body. "Jerry's [Parr] decision to go directly to the hospital was the difference between my dad living and dying," Michael Reagan says in his autobiography, *On The Outside Looking In.*

Michael also says his father told him "that it was only divine intervention that kept him alive."

John Barletta is a retired Secret Service agent and Presidential Protective Detail commander who was very close to President and Mrs. Reagan. He rode horses with Reagan at the president's ranch. When I was a guest at John Barletta's house for a dinner in 2003, two of his fellow retired Secret Service agent friends had come to town to visit him. What I learned that night about the day President Reagan was shot was amazing—and it confirmed what I had long believed—that divine providence had been involved in the saving of President Reagan's life. I sat at the dinner table spellbound as agent Will Slade told us about how it could have easily been another agent with the president that day, but because the other agent had a lot of paperwork to finish, Jerry Parr had offered to go with the president. Will said, "It was a good thing that Jerry was there with the president at the shooting because he was a very experienced agent. He helped save the president's life."

THE PRESIDENT'S PRAYER

When President Reagan was waiting to be taken into the operating room, he could see that White House Press Secretary Jim Brady was unconscious while being wheeled into surgery. Reagan says, "Someone told me he was hit so badly he probably wouldn't make it, and I quickly said a prayer for him. I didn't feel I could ask God's help to heal Jim, the others, and myself, and at the same time feel hatred for the man who had shot us, so I silently asked God to help him deal with whatever demons had led him to shoot us." He also said, "That day, I asked the Lord to heal him, and to this day, I still do."

After hearing from his support staffers what the Secret Service agents, Jerry Parr and Tim McCarthy, had done to save his life, Reagan says, "I thanked God for what He and they had done for me." He continues, "Even with all the protection in the world, I'd thought it was probably impossible to guarantee completely the safety of the president. Now I'd not only benefited from the selflessness of these two men; God, for some reason, had seen fit to give me his blessing and allow me to live a while longer."

Only twelve days after the shooting, President Reagan went home to the White House—an amazing recovery time considering his age and the fact that he had developed a virulent staph infection four days after surgery and had almost died from it, according to his close friend Ed Meese. An article published in the *Washington Post* quoted some of the physicians who had treated him, noting, "All of his physicians agreed that President Reagan was among the most resilient of patients they have ever encountered."

Reagan's rapid recovery, wit, and good sense of humor displayed throughout the ordeal helped allay the fears of the American public when they heard the horrible news. After his wife Nancy had rushed to the hospital to see him, he joked, "Honey, I forgot to duck." When James Baker, chief of staff, and Ed Meese, counselor to the president, were first spotted by Reagan prior to his surgery, he quipped, "Who's minding the store?" According to Mike Deaver, his comment drew collective but nervous laughter from his advisers.

Dr. Aaron visited his patient at the White House after he returned home. The Secret Service agents informed him that the president was making incredible progress recovering and was "itchin'" to go back to his ranch in California. They both agreed that it was by God's grace in answer to the prayers of the president, his wife Nancy, Dr. Aaron, and millions of American citizens that the president was still alive.

President Reagan spoke about those prayers when he said, "It's a remarkable feeling to know that people are praying for you and for your strength. I know firsthand. I felt those prayers when I was recovering from that bullet."

Recovering in the White House, President Reagan recommitted his life to God, writing in his diary, "Whatever happens now, I owe my life to God and will try to serve him in every way I can."

In her book, *When Character Was King,* Peggy Noonan tells of a conversation she had with Mike Deaver about the president. He told her, "I know from conversations he and I had after the assassination attempt that there was no question in his mind that his life had been spared. He absolutely believed it. He felt the Lord had spared him to fulfill whatever mission it was that he was supposed to fulfill. And he was gonna make sure that he lived his life to the fullest and did whatever he considered to be the right thing for the rest of his life."

On the morning of Good Friday, just a few weeks after the attempt on his life, Reagan told Deaver that he'd like to see a man of the cloth. His own pastor, Donn Moomaw of Bel Air Presbyterian Church, was unavailable, so Deaver called Cardinal Terence J. Cooke, whom Reagan knew as a friend. The two men met for nearly an hour, and toward the end of their conversation Cooke told the president that "the hand of God was upon him." President Reagan agreed. "I know, I have decided that whatever time I may have left is left for Him," said the president.

This near-death experience had changed Ronald Reagan in profound ways, and the world would soon feel the impact.

Nelle Reagan, my mother, God rest her soul, had an unshakable faith in God's goodness. And while I may have not realized it in my youth, I know now that she planted that faith very deeply in me. She made the most difficult Christian message seem very easy.

—RONALD REAGAN

CHAPTER 2

NELLE REAGAN: BUILDING YOUNG REAGAN'S ROCK OF FAITH

Train up a child in the way he should go,
and when he is old he will not depart from it.

PROVERBS 22:6

T he key to understanding Ronald Reagan is to look back at his childhood and learn about his mother, Nelle Wilson Reagan. Without a doubt, she was the most influential person in his life; what she taught him when he was young remained with him throughout his life. Years after her death, Reagan would quote her, and her guiding principles became his own. The time, investment, and strong faith that she poured into his life are what produced one of America's greatest presidents. *Presidential Passions* author Michael John Sullivan describes her as "an extraordinary woman who appears to have possessed only positive traits. She was an almost ideal mother in her ability to nurture her son and bring out his best qualities while at the same time instilling her own high values and principles."

She was an amazing Christian woman whom President Reagan credits for truly influencing him and his brother Neil. In 1981, Reagan said, "There is no institution more vital to our nation's survival than the American family. Here the seeds of personal character are planted, the roots of public virtue first nourished. Through love and instruction, discipline, guidance and example, we learn from our mothers and fathers the values that will shape our private lives and our public citizenship."

Nelle Reagan had a powerful faith in God, and she possessed a giving and kind nature. In *An American Life*, Reagan describes his mother and her philosophy toward life: "I was raised to believe that God has a plan for everyone and that seemingly random twists of fate are all a part of His plan. My mother—a small woman with auburn hair and a sense of optimism that ran as deep as the cosmos—told me that everything in life happened for a purpose. She said all things were part of God's Plan, even the most disheartening setbacks, and in the end, she said, you didn't let it get you down: You stepped away from it, stepped over it, and moved on. Later on, she added, something good will happen and you'll find yourself thinking—'If I hadn't had that problem back then, then this better thing that *did* happen wouldn't have happened to me.'"

His mother's words came true time and time again, just as Nelle said they would, as miraculous turns of events allowed Reagan to see God's intervention and plans for his life.

HUMBLE BEGINNINGS

Ronald Wilson Reagan was born on February 6, 1911, to Nelle Wilson Reagan and John Edward ("Jack") Reagan in Tampico, Illinois. On that day, the local newspaper, the *Tampicio Tornado*, reported that "[o]ne of the worst blizzards occurred late Sunday [February 5, 1911]. After the wind and snow had spent its fury, the snow was ten inches to a foot on the level and drifted badly making the highways nearly impassable." Jack feared for Nelle's life because she was having a difficult time in hard labor. After their two-year-old son Neil was taken to a neighbor's house, Jack made his way through the deep snow to the doctor's house. When he arrived, Jack found that the doctor was out on another house call. Jack then trudged back out into the snow to the local midwife's house. Fortunately, she was available to help. After Jack made it back home with the midwife, Nelle went through a long and painful labor before finally giving birth. The doctor eventually arrived but not before Ronald Reagan was born.

"He looks like a fat little Dutchman," Jack is reported to have said about the arrival of his ten-pound baby boy, "but who knows, he might grow up to be president some day." The nickname "Dutch," which his father gave him that very day, would stay with Reagan throughout his childhood and early adulthood, until he went to Hollywood and decided "Dutch" would not be a good name for a movie star.

Nelle's assessment of her new son was summed up in these words, "I think he's perfectly wonderful." She named him "Ronald Wilson Reagan," giving him her maiden name, Wilson. (It's interesting to note that a high percentage of American presidents have had their mother's maiden name as their middle name—evidence, perhaps, of a mother's powerful influence on the lives and successes of great men.)

After the birth, the doctor told Nelle that she should not have any more children since she had experienced such a difficult delivery. Despite her initial disappointment, she followed his advice and never bore another child.

Nellie Clyde Wilson was born on July 24, 1883, the youngest of seven children. Later, she would change her name to Nelle because she thought it had a more theatrical flair. The descendants of Scotch-English ancestors, the Wilson family were religious people who regularly attended church. Nelle had a detailed knowledge of the Bible even as a child. And alcohol was only used for medicinal, sacramental, or ceremonial occasions in the Wilson household—never for pleasure.

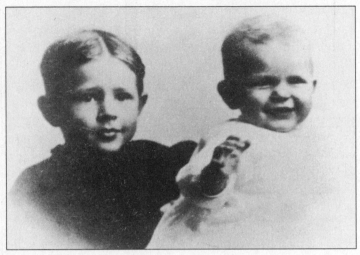

Ronald Reagan and his older brother Neil (Moon) had a close relationship. The two are seen here in a photo circa 1912. (Courtesy of the Ronald Reagan Library)

In Jack Reagan's family, however, the consumption of alcohol was part and partial to their raucous way of life. The Reagans had come from Ireland to Illinois before the Civil War, and Jack's family, all practicing Catholics, loved to dance reels and jigs. They also consumed large quantities of corn whiskey—to the Reagan men, drinking hard without getting drunk was a test of a man's character and showed his self control.

Jack was also born in the year 1883, but his family life was full of tragedy. Jack's parents died of tuberculosis when he was only six years old. An elderly aunt took over his guardianship and "raised him a proper Irish Catholic." At the age of sixteen, Jack settled in a town called Fulton, Illinois, where he got a job selling shoes in a local store. Shortly thereafter, a lovely young girl came to work there, too. Her name was Nelle.

With dark, handsome looks, a muscular build, and a way with words, Jack quickly won Nelle's heart. Jack could tell a wonderful story, and his charms probably would have attracted any young girl, but, even at this young age, he had developed a reputation for drinking too much alcohol.

Still, Nelle, who sported a petite frame, bright blue eyes, and auburn hair, was a romantic. She fell head over heels in love with Jack Reagan. Fortunately, Nelle was a kind, forgiving soul as well as a lovely face, and she would learn to forgive much during the years she was married to Jack.

The couple married on November 4, 1904, in the parsonage of the Immaculate Conception Catholic Church. It was here that Jack had occasionally attended Mass.

The couple's first son, John Neil Reagan, was born on September 16, 1908, in a home birth. Shortly after his birth, Neil was baptized at the Catholic church, which came as a complete surprise to Nelle, who had grown up as a Protestant. The priest had not told Nelle that he expected that their children would be raised in the Catholic faith.

Although she had been brought up going to church and reading the Bible as a child, something miraculous happened to Nelle a year before her son Ronald was born, and it changed her life forever. Nelle had a genuine conversion experience, and she became a deeply committed Christian. She became what many would call a "born-again Christian." Soon after this deepening of her faith, she was baptized by immersion in water. She now publicly professed her faith in Christ, and she became a member of the Christian Church in Tampico, Illinois. The Christian Church, later known as the Disciples of Christ, was an offshoot of the Presbyterian Church, and professed the simple gospel, seeking unity among Christians. It suited Nelle well because it strongly supported education and literary pursuits and encouraged good works.

LEARNING THE VALUE OF HARD WORK, EDUCATION, AND CULTURE

Dutch loved his father dearly. He was proud of his father's Irish-Catholic heritage and admired his solid work ethic. "My dad believed passionately in the rights of the individual and the working man," President Reagan would later recall. "Among the things he passed on to me were the belief that all men and women, regardless of their color or religion, are created equal and that individuals determine their own destiny; that is, it's largely their own ambition and hard work that determine their fate in life."

Reagan sums up the differences in his parents this way: "While my father was a cynic and tended to suspect the worst of people, my mother was the opposite. She always expected to find the best in people and often did, even among the prisoners at our local jail to whom she frequently brought hot meals.

"I learned from my father the value of hard work and ambition, and maybe a little something about telling a story. From my mother, I learned the value of prayer, how to have dreams and believe I could make them come true. Although my father's attendance at Catholic Mass was sporadic, my mother seldom missed Sunday services at the Disciples of Christ church in Dixon."

Reagan continues, "While my father was filled with dreams of making something of himself, she had a drive to help my brother and me make something of ourselves."

Nelle's motto was "To higher, nobler things my mind is bent," and she loved books, poetry, dramatic arts, and the Bible. Nelle was the one who encouraged her sons to go to college at a time when very few young people pursued a college degree. President Reagan once said, "In the 1920s, fewer than seven percent of the high school graduates in America went to college, but I was determined to be among them."

Jack had told his sons that if they wanted a college education, they would have to earn the money to pay for it themselves. But Dutch was determined to do it. So determined in fact that he held full-time summer jobs from the age of fourteen to save money for his college tuition.

While Dutch was learning the importance of hard work, his mother was teaching him other valuable life lessons, including lessons about manners. Nelle was always looking for ways to improve herself and her children. One thing she taught Dutch was to "look people straight in the eye" when talking to them. She also taught him such commonsense advice as "remember people's names and let them know you care." Nelle raised young Dutch to be gracious to everyone and to always use good manners. In fact, she was so well versed in etiquette she could have written a book on manners or probably taught etiquette classes. Through her teachings, Dutch learned to stand when a woman entered a room and to tip his hat and carry heavy packages for ladies. As a teenager, he picked up the habit of always saying "God bless you" instead of "goodbye." Reagan would use this same phrase when ending his speeches as president.

A BRUSH WITH DEATH

When Dutch was three months old, his family moved to what was called Burden House, a house that was small but did have an indoor toilet and plumbing, unlike the five-room apartment where Reagan was born. The house faced a park that featured a Civil War cannon with cannon balls stacked next to it. And beyond the park, on the other side, were railroad tracks where, as young boys, Dutch and Neil nearly lost their lives.

This near-tragic episode began on a hot Illinois day when five-year-old Neil spotted an ice wagon stopped at the train depot near the park. He quickly devised a plan to steal some of the shaved ice from the back of the ice wagon. Dutch, who was only three years old at the time, followed behind his big brother. Together, they crawled under a huge freight train, just as the train was about to pull away from the depot. As if divinely prompted, the young boys scampered out from beneath the train just in time to avoid the massive wheels, which would have certainly crushed the boys to death. Nelle came out onto the porch just in time to witness this near-tragedy.

President Reagan said his mother ran over to them at the ice wagon and "earlifted us home." One cannot help but wonder if God spared young Dutch that day because He had a special plan for Reagan's life.

Young Dutch had other narrow escapes from death, including a near-fatal car accident. "We were riding in one of those old original Ford touring cars, with the brass radiator and lamps," the president recalls in Frank van der Linden's *The Real Reagan*. "It had to be a neighbor's car, or a relative's, because it was a long time before we owned one. The car tipped over. Everybody got out all right except me. I was still underneath. They fished me out from under the car." Amazingly enough, he was unharmed.

JACK REAGAN'S WANDERING WAYS

The Reagan family moved often, at least ten times while Ronald Reagan was growing up. In fact, they always rented and never owned a house. Many of these moves were the result of Jack's being fired from a job because of his drinking problems. On other occasions, they moved because Jack was always looking for jobs with brighter prospects. But as one of the millions living through the Depression, Jack had trouble getting work and supporting his family in those tough economic times.

Through all these difficult trials, however, Nelle continued in her positive attitude toward life and grew stronger in her faith. Neil once said about his mother, "[She] was the one where come rent day and my Dad would say, 'Nellie the rent is due day after tomorrow,' my mother would just look at him and say, 'Don't worry, the Lord will provide.'" And the Lord did provide. Nelle would take in sewing or rent out one of their rooms to supplement Jack's wages, and they would miraculously make it through the month. Sometimes, when they didn't know where their next meal was coming from, someone would secretly drop off a dish of food for the Reagans while they were away from home. The Reagans' anonymous benefactors were generously repaying Nelle for her kindnesses to them. When President Reagan recalled his childhood, he said that he never knew until later in life that they were poor.

One of Dutch's favorite dishes that his mother often made was called "Oatmeal Meat." The recipe was simple: She would take hamburger and mix it with oatmeal, fry it, and then make gravy from the meat. President Reagan says, "It makes the meat go a long way. I thought it was a luxury.

Ronald Reagan (with "Dutch" haircut), Neil Reagan, and parents Jack and Nelle Reagan in Tampico, Illinois, on a family Christmas card, circa 1916–17. (Courtesy of the Ronald Reagan Library)

I loved it." Nelle served large quantities of oatmeal as well as soup at the Reagan home. The president also reflected on this, "We always had enough to eat and Nelle was forever finding people who were worse off than we were. When she found the less fortunate she was forever going out of her way to help them." According to Reagan, "I can see her now with a dish and a towel over the dish, taking food to a family that didn't have anything to eat." Even in difficult times, Nelle tithed to her church, and she taught her boys to do so, too. She would oppose Jack whenever he complained about it, telling him, "The Lord [will] make your ninety percent twice as big if you [make] sure He [gets] his tenth." President Reagan would tithe throughout his life. In regards to saving for college, he said, "Ever since I'd begun working with a pick and shovel, I'd bank just about everything I earned except for the church tithe, my mother called 'The Lord's Share.'"

Despite the hard times, Nelle was prudent with what little money they did have. She always made sure that her boys had what she thought was important in life.

NELLE'S POWERFUL INFLUENCE

Every week, Nelle took her sons to Sunday school and, when they were older, to the Sunday church service. The boys also attended prayer meetings with their mother on Wednesday and Sunday evenings. Prayer was an important part of Nelle's life, and she prayed with and for many people. One friend remarked, when Nelle prayed it was like she had a direct connection to God.

President Reagan was also a firm believer in the power of prayer. He once said, "I've always believed that we were, each of us, put here for a reason; that there is a plan, somehow divine for all of us. In an effort to embrace that plan, we are blessed with the special gift of prayer, the happiness and solace to be gained by talking to the Lord. It is our hopes and our aspirations, our sorrows and fears, our deep remorse and renewed resolve, our thanks and joyful praise, and most especially our love, all turned towards a loving God.

"Many of us have been taught to pray by people we love. In my case, it was my mother. I learned quite literally at her knee.

"My mother gave me a great deal, but nothing she gave me was more important than that. She was my inspiration and provided me with a very real and deep faith."

Despite their frequent moves and hard times, the Reagan boys always had their mother Nelle as a constant. She gave them both unconditional love with a combination of encouragement and discipline.

Nelle also gave her sons an important advantage in life: She taught them how to read and how to love reading. When Ronald Reagan was governor of California, he wrote a letter to a woman telling her, "I'm one of those who remembers vividly the magic of a library. Thank heaven, I learned of the exciting world to be found in books and that excitement remains." And then he quoted one of his mother's sayings, "No one can be lonely who has a book for company."

President Reagan describes how he learned to read at age five even before he started school: "My mother always came into our room at bedtime and wedged herself between my brother and me to read us a story. As she read, she followed each line on the page with her finger and we watched, I think I just picked it up that way."

Nelle often read to the boys stories about good and evil and how the good guy had the courage to do the right thing. Sometimes the hero in the story was a knight in shining armor, willing to fight for God and the king. Many of the stories had great moral lessons, and it was through literature that she often taught them her principles and values. One of her favorite themes in books and plays was that of the eventual triumph of good over evil. This theme was later to be played out in President Reagan's presidency with his "Evil Empire" speech and the eventual downfall of communism. Other recurrent themes included those of noble people willing to do great things. The themes of these stories remained etched in Dutch's mind. In 1973, when Reagan was governor of California, he said: "The history of our civilization, the great advances that made it possible, is not a story of cynics or doom criers. It is a gallant chronicle of the optimists, the determined people, men and women, who dreamed great dreams and dared to try whatever it took to make them come true."

At the kitchen table, Nelle often helped her sons with homework and taught them from the Bible while Jack read the newspaper. With her sons nestled up next to her eating popcorn or apples, Nelle would read them stories about King Arthur and the Knights of the Round Table or the Three Musketeers. When Dutch's cat had kittens, he named them King Arthur, Sir Galahad, and Buster. And Nelle was not just a talker about good deeds. She put her faith into action. President Reagan called her "a do gooder." Today, this term has a negative connotation, but Reagan meant it as a high compliment. Nelle took to heart the Bible verse in Galatians 6:9 which urges Christians to "not grow weary while doing good, for in due season we shall reap if we do not lose heart," as well as James 2:17, which reads, "Thus also faith by itself, if it does not have works, is dead." She was continually helping someone in need, including prisoners in the local jail, or taking food to others when they were sick and praying with them. In her book *Young Reagan*, Anne Edwards says of Nelle, "She had a melodious voice, an ability to speak with conviction and she could quote the Bible at length." She continues, "When words of comfort or hope were needed, she always knew the right and meaningful passage."

A lovely old hymn, "Brighten the Corner Where You Are," which was written around this time of Nelle's life, captures her essence:

> Do not wait until some *deed* of greatness you may do;
> Do not wait to shed your light afar.
> To the many duties ever near you now be true.
> Brighten the corner where you are.

FACING BIGOTRY

The frequent moves were hard on Dutch and later proved to impact his personal relationships. Although he was able to make friends, he had trouble getting close to people because he was always having to say goodbye. Dutch was also teased by other children in school because he was from an Irish Catholic family. In reality, he belonged to a religiously divided family, but because his name was Reagan and because there was strong anti-Catholic sentiment during the early twentieth century, he saw the worst side of religious bigotry. He got into many a fistfight with other children over this anti-Catholic teasing.

Anne Edwards tells how one woman who attended school with Reagan described him on his first day at school: "He was startling to look at (not only good-looking but he had this air about him), and [my friend Laura] sensed that he was special and should be introduced. I sensed it, too, and used to turn around in class just to stare back at him. His jaw was always set—as though somebody was going to take a poke at him and he was ready for the punches . . . I looked at his thrust out chin every day and wondered 'Why?'"

Dutch's parents constantly instructed their sons about "the importance of judging people as *individuals*." They would not allow any racial or religious intolerance in their home, probably because Jack had been subjected to it so much for being an Irish Catholic. According to President Reagan, Nelle taught her children to "Treat thy neighbor as you would want your neighbor to treat you." This was Nelle's version of the classic "Golden Rule." She also was fond of saying, "Judge everyone by how they act, not what they are."

NELLE NEARLY DIES

When Dutch was just seven years old, his mother had a near-death experience that deepened her faith and impacted the rest of her life. That year, 1918, the world was hit by a pandemic of a very deadly strain of influenza. Over five hundred thousand lives were lost in the United States, and twenty million died worldwide. Schools were closed, and everyone wore masks to avoid coming down with this deadly disease. Despite these safety measures, however, Nelle contracted the virus and nearly died.

According to President Reagan's daughter, Maureen, Nelle later described "in vivid detail the phenomenon common to others who come back from the brink: The memory of being bathed in a brilliant light, the feeling of floating, the awareness that she was dying." Jack knelt and prayed at her bedside and burned altar candles at church, doing everything he knew to save her life. The family doctor was called, and Dutch watched "the guy with the black bag" walk outside the house to talk to Jack about the possibility of losing Nelle. Reagan remembers going to bed each night with "a weight dragging at the pit of my stomach till one day Jack said 'she's going to be all right,' and his face looked as if the sun was out."

The doctor had told Jack to feed Nelle moldy, green cheese—the moldier the better—even though, in 1918, penicillin and its connection to mold had not yet been discovered. Despite heavy odds, Nelle recovered. The family's prayers had been answered.

In 1920, the Reagan family moved to Dixon, Illinois. Dutch was just nine years old at the time, and to him the small town of less than ten thousand people "was heaven." President Reagan writes in *An American Life*, "It was a small universe where I learned standards and values that would guide me for the rest of my life."

At the First Christian Church of Dixon, Nelle was made the teacher of the "True Blue" Sunday school class, a class that was composed of about twenty-five women who met either at Nelle's house or at the church to read and study the Bible and where each lady would share how God had helped them through their ups and downs in life. When the group met at the Reagan's house, Dutch would often join them. The ladies in the class absolutely adored Nelle, and she was so highly regarded that she remained the teacher of the class until the Reagans departed for Hollywood, California, in September of 1937.

AN ADDICTION TO ALCOHOL

When Dutch was only eleven, he experienced a horrifying incident with his dad that would be forever emblazoned in his memory. It happened on a cold and blustery winter night. Nelle was out of the house on a sewing job, and when the young Reagan returned home he "nearly stumbled over a lump near the front door; it was Jack lying in the snow, his arms outstretched, flat on his back. I leaned over to see what was wrong and smelled whiskey." Dutch couldn't wake him—Jack just kept snoring—and so Dutch "grabbed a piece of his overcoat, pulled it, and dragged him into the house, then put him to bed and never mentioned it to my mother." Although his mother did not know about this incident, she was fully aware of Jack's problem with alcohol and its effect on the family. When Reagan's mother thought the boys were old enough, she sat them down and explained why their father sometimes disappeared. According to Reagan, she told them that "Jack had a sickness that he couldn't control—an addiction to alcohol" and they "shouldn't love him any less because of it."

Even through the difficult times with Jack's alcoholism, his "bouts with the dark demon in the bottle," and living on a bare existence worsened by Jack's frequent unemployment and irresponsible spending habits, Nelle maintained her positive attitude and kept believing that things would get better. President Reagan remembers his mother's steadfast love and commitment in those hard years: "My mother would pray constantly for [my father]. She was on her knees several times a day. And she refused to give up, no matter how dark things looked."

Nelle Reagan's secret recipe for life could be aptly summed up in I Thessalonians 5:16–18: "Rejoice always, pray without ceasing, in everything give thanks; for this is the will of God in Christ Jesus for you." She remained thankful and optimistic in all circumstances and constantly turned to the Lord in prayer, sustaining an intimate relationship with Him. Putting her faith and trust in the Lord in her hardest times, she turned to God's Word and believed it. God was her rock and fortress, and she clung to His promises.

DUTCH'S BAPTISM

When Dutch was only twelve years old, his mother gave him a book entitled *That Printer of Udell's* by Harold Bell Wright. Reagan later declared that this book, which he described as "a wonderful book about a devout itinerant Christian," changed his life. The story follows Dick, a young man who leaves home after his mother has died and he is left to cope with his alcoholic father. As Dick deals with the tragedies in his life, he learns what true and sincere Christianity really means. The book ends with Dick praying with his wife and leaving a good job "to enter a field of wider usefulness in the nation's Capital" as a congressman and concludes with this quote from Jesus: "Inasmuch as ye have done it unto one of the least of these, my brethren, ye have done it unto Me." After finishing *That Printer of Udell's*, Reagan went to his mother and said, "I want to be like that man," and he subsequently made his decision to commit his life to Christ, to be baptized, and to officially join his mother's church, the Disciples of Christ.

Dutch invited his brother Neil to be baptized with him, and, on June 21, 1922, the two Reagan boys were baptized along with twenty-three other individuals at First Christian Church in Dixon, Illinois.

AN INTRODUCTION TO THEATER

In addition to her church activities and sewing jobs, one of Nelle's favorite hobbies was acting and giving dramatic readings. She had a wonderfully dynamic voice, which could be used as an instrument to convey a striking variety of emotions. President Reagan recalls that she "executed it with the zest of a frustrated actress" and "recited classic speeches in tragic tones, wept as she flung herself into the more poignant passages . . . and poured out poetry by the yard." She acted in plays that she wrote for her church, most of which included a solid moral lesson, and even penned a number of poems for the local paper inviting people to come to Sunday school. She also got her sons involved, casting them in featured roles.

Nelle gave Dutch his first try at acting when he was about nine years old. At first, she had to encourage her timid little boy to try it, but once he actually performed and got a taste of the applause, young Dutch really enjoyed it. She instilled in him a love of drama that began with small plays in childhood, led through both high school and college drama clubs, and of course took him all the way to Hollywood where he spent decades as a successful actor.

What often comes as a surprise to those who don't know President Reagan is that he is actually shy and introverted. His favorite activities as a child were reading and watching movies. He spent hours upon hours reading and re-reading his favorite books, such as *Northern Trails*, with tales about Alaska and the Arctic, and stories about Tom Swift, the young adventurer and inventor. Reagan was also drawn to books about outer space and nature. These books instilled in him a lifelong interest in space, an interest that culminated in his involvement in the space program while serving as president. And the movies young Reagan enjoyed were about cowboy heroes who got the girl after defeating the bad guys. As a result of this fascination with cowboys, Reagan began riding horses as an adult and had several ranches that he treasured. On these ranches, he became a real-life cowboy and lived out some of the adventures he saw in the movies as a child.

Brother Neil, though, was the opposite of Dutch. He was an extrovert, outgoing and exuberant. But Neil also had a pessimistic attitude and was, in fact, much more like his father, while Dutch was like his mother. As an adult, Neil often reflected on how hard times were and how poor the family was—in contrast to Dutch who said he never knew they were poor and therefore had a much more romantic picture of their childhood.

Reagan writes in his autobiography about the time when, after moving into a new house, he found a box in the attic, left there from a previous occupant. Inside the box was a huge collection of birds' eggs and butterflies displayed in a glass case. Reagan says he spent many hours "marveling at the rich colors of the eggs and the intricate and fragile wings of the butterflies." This experience left him throughout his life "with a reverence for the handiwork of God."

CHARACTER FIT FOR A PRESIDENT

Nelle Reagan played a tremendous role in developing Ronald Reagan's character, principles, and beliefs. She raised him to be a man of convictions, to always do the right thing and to persevere to the end. Most of all, she shared with her son her faith in a good and loving God who has a purpose and plan for our lives. President Reagan's long-time secretary, Helene von Damm, who worked for Reagan from the time he was governor of California until his presidency, had an intimate knowledge of his character and beliefs and, several years ago, edited a book of letters that then-Governor Reagan had written in response to correspondence he had received. She would attest in her book that Reagan had received from his mother the "Christian beliefs that even today strongly mark his letters, his conversations, his speeches, and his actions." With traditional values and strong principles, Nelle laid a firm foundation and nurtured him to become a great man and eventually a great president.

Parents—especially mothers—have an awesome job and responsibility. It's not just a cliché that the hand that rocks the cradle rules the world. Any parent may be raising tomorrow's president. And although Jack's influence and impact on young Reagan can't be overestimated— he did give Dutch a strong work ethic, making him work at such an early age—it is Nelle's Christian life and maternal skills that serve as the best parental example.

Nancy Reagan once said that Ronald lived by a little saying Nelle had written in her Bible many years ago: "You can be too big for God to use, but you cannot be too small." This simple statement helped remind Reagan of the importance of having a humble servant's heart like his mother's.

President Reagan once said of his mother, "She was the gentlest, the kindest woman that anyone ever knew." On May 7, 1983, he gave a radio address to the nation for Mother's Day. In this address, he paid a stirring tribute to his mother: "In our families, and often from our mothers, we first learn about values and caring and the difference between right and wrong. Those of us blessed with loving families draw our confidence from them and the strength we need to face the world. We also first learn at home, and again, often from our mothers, about the God who will guide us through life.

"Now and then I find guidance and direction in the worn brown Bible I used to take the oath of office. It's been the Reagan family Bible, and, like many of yours, has its flyleaf filled with important events; its margins are scrawled with insights and passages underlined for emphasis. My mother, Nelle, made all those marks in that book. She used it to instruct her two young sons, and I look to it still.

"A passage in Proverbs describes the ideal woman, saying: 'Strength and dignity are her clothing, and she smiles at the future. She opens her mouth in wisdom, and the teaching of kindness is on her tongue. Give her the product of her hands, and let her works praise her in the gates.'

"Well, that passage calls for us to recognize the enormous strengths and contributions of women, wives, and mothers and indicates to me that society always needs a little reminding. Well, let us use this weekend as a symbol that we will always remember, reward, and recognize them and use their examples of love and courage as inspiration to be better than we are."

Reagan biographer and former *Washington Post* reporter Lou Cannon was absolutely right when he said, "You and I would never have heard of Ronald Reagan if it had not been for his mother, Nelle."

There is no institution more vital to our nation's survival than the American family. Here the seeds of personal character are planted, the roots of public virtue first nourished. Through love and instruction, discipline, guidance and example, we learn from our mothers and fathers the values that will shape our private lives and our public citizenship.

The days of our childhood forecast our lives, as poets and philosophers long have told us. "The childhood shows the man as morning shows the day," John Milton wrote. "Train up a child in the way he should go: and when he is old, he will not depart from it," Solomon tells us. Clearly, the future is in the care of our parents.

—RONALD REAGAN

CHAPTER 3

THE HIGH
SCHOOL YEARS

*Honor your father and your mother, that your
days may be long upon the land which the
Lord your God is giving you.*

EXODUS 20:12

The period in life between the innocence of childhood and the full responsibilities of adulthood is a very challenging time. It's a time of struggling through intense and accelerated physical, social, and psychological changes. A time when a person makes decisions that will literally set a course for the rest of his life. A time when young people gain a sense of identity, discovering their personal gifts, interests, and passions.

For Ronald Reagan, it was a time for learning what kind of man he was destined to become. Throughout his teenage and young adult years, the hand of God was evident in Reagan's life as he matured in his faith and found his gifts, interests, and passions through experiences at school, jobs, church, and extracurricular activities, all of which would play an important role in his adulthood. In *An American Life*, Reagan admits that he had insecurities as a child but by the end of his college days had gained a large measure of self-confidence and learned how to set goals for himself, an important development for his future success.

SCHOOL DAYS

At thirteen years of age, Dutch entered Dixon High School. He loved the game of football and desperately wanted to play for the school team. His big brother, now known by his nickname "Moon," was already a star on the team, and this made Dutch want to be on the team even more. When he told his father Jack that he wanted to play football, Jack responded with his typical pessimism by saying, "If you want to do something that foolish, go ahead, but you'll get your neck broken."

Although the high school had only one football team, the school had recently divided into two campuses on opposite sides of town. Moon had started school at the South Side campus and remained there. But the family had moved to the north end of town and Dutch was assigned to the North Side campus. He saw this as a fortunate turn of events because, according to Reagan, "[my brother] always had an outspoken, self-confident personality that was a little like Jack's, which made him a natural leader, and until then I think I probably felt a little under his shadow." Now, without Moon around, young Dutch wouldn't be compared to his big brother, and he could blossom into what God had planned for him to become.

Eager to be on the football team, Dutch showed up for practice ready to play, but he was so small the school had only one special pair of football pants that would fit him—pants that had thigh pads made of bamboo. Standing just five feet three inches tall and weighing a mere 108 pounds, Dutch was a runt on the field and was quickly passed over for bigger boys to fill the team roster. Dutch was sorely disappointed, but this rejection made him all the more determined to try out for the team the next fall. By next summer, he still hadn't grown much, so he took a job to increase his strength as well as make money.

For thirty-five cents an hour, Dutch worked with a pick and shovel to help build and remodel houses. He later said of this work experience, "I learned a lot that summer—how to use my hands, how to lay floors and shingle roofs, and work with concrete." These were skills that he would later use on the ranches he owned. Dutch discovered that summer that he enjoyed working hard and using his hands by doing tough manual labor.

By the time the school year started again, the football conference had instituted a new division for smaller players who weighed up to 135 pounds. Dutch was elected captain of this new team and gained new confidence. By his junior year, Dutch was up to nearly six feet in height and weighed 160 pounds. However, even though he was given a position on the first-string team, he "was still warming the bench." It wasn't until halfway through the season that he was called in to play during a game. He remained on the first string throughout his senior year. Dutch's body had, by then, matured and grown bigger and stronger. He was a late bloomer even through his college days.

After his sophomore year of high school, Dutch was hired as a life-guard—"one of the best jobs I ever had," Reagan says. When Dutch heard that Lowell Park might be closed, due to several tragic drown-ings in the nearby treacherous Rock River, he volunteered to be the lifeguard at the swimming area. Dutch was a strong swimmer and had taken a lifesaving course at the YMCA, and being a lifeguard was a job he earnestly enjoyed. He would eventually work there seven days a week, for a total of seven summers. Nelle would occasionally come out to the park with a picnic lunch and sit on the beach with her friends, enjoy the day, and get a chance to see her son in action. At his father's suggestion, Dutch would cut a notch in one particular old log every time he saved someone's life. By the end of those seven summers, Dutch had etched seventy-seven notches in the log. His employer's wife, Mrs. Graybill, said about him: "He was real pleasant to everybody and treated everybody the same. In the morning, if he had time, he would give small children swimming lessons . . . there was never a basket left at closing time. That meant we had a good lifeguard; there were no bodies at the bottom . . . He was a wonderful, good-natured young man. I never heard him speak one cross word to the bathers. He was a beautiful diver."

Ronald Reagan was a lifeguard for seven summers and called it "one of the best jobs I ever had." Lowell Park, Illinois, 1927. (Courtesy of the Ronald Reagan Library)

Built into Reagan's character was the desire to save people from distress. Whether serving as a local lifeguard, pulling flailing swimmers from tumultuous waters, or as president of the United States, pulling the economy out of a recession or other countries out of the grip of communism, Reagan was always helping others.

DUTCH FALLS IN LOVE

Dutch fell in love for the first time when he was in high school. Her name was Margaret Cleaver—"Mugs," as he affectionately called her. She was the daughter of the new minister at his church, and she reminded him of his mother. Reagan describes her as "short, pretty, auburn haired, and intelligent." He goes on to say, "For almost six years of my life I was sure she was going to be my wife. I was very much in love. She was the first girl I ever kissed."

Biographer Anne Edwards writes, "His charm was overwhelming, his kindness almost extreme. He always left people with a way of saying, 'God bless you' and made them feel—just maybe—'he had an inside track.' Margaret's father hoped the boy might find his way into the ministry and encouraged him along that route." Dutch was close to Reverend Cleaver and felt he could freely talk to him and ask for his advice. In fact, the reverend became a father figure to him since his own father was at times emotionally absent from his life and still dependent on alcohol. It was Cleaver, not Jack, who taught Dutch how to drive. Dutch's presence was so significant in the Cleaver family that the reverend's wife later attested Reagan "was in our home all the time."

CHRISTIAN ENDEAVOR

On Sunday evenings, Dutch and his brother went to Christian Endeavor, a young people's ministry that met at his church. According to church records at the First Christian Church in Dixon, Illinois, Dutch was seriously involved in Christian Endeavor, and "he obviously was impressed by the work ethic which is interwoven throughout this adjunct to church and Sunday school activities." The church proudly reports on their website, "Apparently [Reagan] was so inspired by these thoughts and beliefs that he carried them throughout his life." This ministry is another important piece—though overlooked until now—in the complex puzzle of Reagan's life, a golden nugget that explains so much about Reagan and why he did what he did in his early years and later while serving as president of the United States.

The Christian Endeavor association is a Christ-centered ministry that was started in 1881. It is interdenominational and has spread across America as well as the rest of the world. The purpose of Christian Endeavor is to strengthen the spiritual life and promote Christian activities among its members. According to its own mission, the association "provides for the training and development of the people of the church to minister in their church, home, work and wherever else they choose." While a typical Sunday school's purpose is to teach, Christian Endeavor's purpose is to encourage the open expression of Christian faith through actions and good deeds. The ministry strengthens the local church by equipping its youth and adults for Christian service and leadership.

The First Christian Church in Dixon understandably believes that this group, Christian Endeavor, played a pivotal role in inspiring President Reagan throughout his life and reported that it "is humbly and respectfully proud to have played some small part in the nurturing and Christian training of a youth who was later to hold the highest office in the United States, and arguably, the most important governmental position in the world!"

Dutch also occasionally led prayer meetings at church. Members of his church enjoyed listening to Dutch's dynamic, engaging voice and delivery, which was most likely the result of the elocution (the art of public speaking) lessons that his mother gave him. Some church members later remarked how Dutch would make the Bible seem personal and alive, as if the "phrase might just have been written."

Dutch was an active Christian throughout his youth and served in many roles at his home church in Dixon. As a teen, Dutch began teaching Sunday school for younger boys at his church, using Christian athletes as role models for his students. In 1926, while still in high school, he led an Easter sunrise service and even continued his teaching duties after he had started college, returning to Dixon on the weekends.

Dutch's brother Neil, though, found a church home elsewhere in the town. Although Dutch and Neil were both taken to the First Christian Church (Disciples of Christ) by their mother, Neil eventually began attending Mass with his father in his mid-teens. At eighteen, Neil decided to become a Catholic like his father and was surprised to find out that he had already been baptized as a Catholic when he was a baby. Nelle believed that each person should have the freedom to determine his or her own faith and never pressured her sons into joining her church. And it was obvious that Neil had much more in common with his father. So Neil joined the Catholic Church, became a regular, like his father, at Knights of Columbus (an international society for Roman Catholic men) events, and remained a practicing, churchgoing Catholic until his death in 1996. The Reagan family was divided religiously, but they were accepting of each other's beliefs, and it was in this tolerant environment that Dutch learned how to be understanding of other people's faith.

DUTCH LEARNS TO ACT

Dutch was involved in many activities in high school, including track, football, basketball, HI-Y (which had as its aim to promote "Clean Speech, Clean Sports, Clean Living and Clean Scholarship"), and drawing and writing for the school yearbook. He also served as president of the student body and, what should come as no surprise, was heavily involved in the drama club and the high school's plays.

Although Nelle had introduced him to drama, Reagan credits his English teacher, B.J. Frazer, for teaching him the "things about acting that stayed with me for the rest of my life." He said by the time he was a senior "I was too addicted to student theatrical productions that you couldn't keep me out of them." Reagan was fortunate to have such a good teacher, one who was amazingly astute about the theater—especially considering that he was attending a school in the middle of rural Illinois. B.J. Frazer taught the students the process of empathy, which Reagan says "is not bad training for someone who goes into politics (or any other calling)." He also says in regards to the virtues of learning to empathize with others, "By developing a knack for putting yourself in someone else's shoes, it helps you relate better to others and perhaps understand why they think as they do, even though they come from a background much different from yours."

Dutch was also a writer and illustrator, and his high school yearbook, *The Dixonian,* displayed examples of his writing and drawing abilities at age seventeen. One of his stories, entitled "Gethsemane" (which is the name of the garden where Jesus was betrayed and went through extreme agony the night before His death), was about a football game. Dutch's story begins with these words, "To every man comes Gethsemane! Some fight the battle surrounded by prison walls, but for all the soul is laid bare. Some fight the battle when old age is creeping on like a silent clinging vine. This is the story of a boy who fought his Gethsemane on the level sward [grassy turf] in the shadow of a deserted grandstand." He ends the story with these words, "And when a friend asked the coach whether he considered the past season successful or not, he thought of the greatest halfback and murmured to himself, 'It matters not that you won or lost, but how you played the game.'"

Dutch also wrote a poem entitled "Life" that appeared in the school annual. The poem serves as a reminder to Christians that we are here on earth for a brief time but are promised eternal life in heaven. It urges us to keep things in perspective and not complain about small problems. This is that poem written by Reagan while still in his teens:

LIFE

I wonder what it's all about, and why
We suffer so, when little things go wrong?
We make our life a struggle,
When life should be a song.

Our troubles break and drench us.
Like spray on the cleaving prow
Of some trim Gloucester schooner,
As it dips in a graceful bow . . .

But why does sorrow drench us
When our fellow passes on?
He's just exchanged life's dreary dirge
For an eternal life of song . . .

Millions have gone before us.
And millions will come behind,
So why do we curse and fight
At a fate both wise and kind?

We hang onto a jaded life
A life full of sorrow and pain.
A life that warps and breaks us,
And we try to run through it again.

As student body president, Dutch spoke at his graduation and quoted John 10:10: "I have come that they may have life, and that they may have *it* more abundantly." In this passage, Jesus promises a life that is not vain and hollow but is brimming with vitality. Christ offers the believer an authentic spiritual existence that will transform him completely and satisfy him forever. Ronald Reagan clearly understood the truths that the path of Christ, though difficult at times, is infinitely rewarding and that a fulfilling and purposeful life is found only in a personal relationship with Him.

When speaking to a group of ministers in 1984, President Reagan said, "You may remember, but I'm sure you don't agree with, a very cynical quote that got wide circulation, from H.L. Mencken. He said Puritanism 'is the haunting fear that someone, somewhere, may be happy.' Well, some suspect that today's spiritual awakening reflects such narrow-mindedness. We must show that faith and traditional values are the things that give life human dignity, warmth, vitality, and yes, laughter and joy. . . . Now, although millions of Americans have already done so much to put our national life back on the firm foundation of faith and traditional values, we still have far to go."

Revealing his bursting optimism, even at the age of seventeen, Dutch wrote in his senior year high school annual: "Life is just one grand sweet song, so start the music." And that's just what he did as he left high school and entered college.

[I]f I had to do it over again, I'd go back to Eureka or another small college like it in a second. . . . There may be a lot to be said for those large institutions, but I think too many young people overlook the value of a small college and the tremendous influence that participation in student activities can have during the years from adolescence to adulthood. . . . If I had gone to one of those larger schools, I think I would have fallen back in the crowd and never discovered things about myself that I did at Eureka. My life would have been different.

—RONALD REAGAN

CHAPTER 4

THE QUIET FAITH
OF RONALD REAGAN

For I know the thoughts that I think toward you,
says the Lord, thoughts of peace and not of evil,
to give you a future and a hope.

JEREMIAH 29:11

Going off to college, Ronald Reagan started a new stanza in the sweet, melodious song of his life. His brother Neil had already decided that going to college "was a waste of time; also an impossibility," and their father Jack had told them both they would have to pay for their college tuition themselves because he couldn't afford to help them. But going to college was a dream for Dutch Reagan, and he was determined to find a way to get there. His girlfriend Margaret was attending Eureka College, a liberal arts institution affiliated with the Disciples of Christ. This, of course, was the denomination that Dutch had attended in Dixon. What's more, one of his high school football heroes had gone on to play football at the very same university.

The school was founded on February 6 (coincidently Reagan's birthday) in 1855. It was a solid, biblically-based Christian school. Eureka's 1871 catalog stated: "The Bible is a regular textbook, and every student may prepare and recite a lesson in it at least once a week. While everything of a sectarian or denominational tendency is conscientiously excluded, it is designed to enforce the sublime morality of the Divine Volume." And in the 1936 catalog, the school continued to maintain its Christian principles, stating: "Religious values shall be found in courses of study, in the work plan, and in recreational activities. The development of religious attitude is essential."

Eureka College had a tremendous impact on President Reagan, and it reinforced his Christian philosophies and beliefs. It was a good "fit" for him, as he later wrote: "It seemed to me then, as I walked up the path, to be another home." On October 17, 1980, Reagan returned to Eureka College and spoke to the student body, praising the benefits of a small, church-related school. He said large universities could provide a good education, but at Eureka, "You will have memories; you will have friendships that are impossible on those great campuses and that just are peculiar to this place."

College is a critical time in a person's life, when he or she will be influenced immeasurably by friends and professors. And it is abundantly clear that Ronald Reagan's views and life were shaped and supported by his Christian upbringing and education. Many years later, as governor of California, he wrote in response to a constituent: "If one book had to be recommended or chosen for life of exile on the proverbial island, I think the Bible would be the unquestioned choice. I know of no other book that could be read and reread and continue to be a challenge as could the Old and New Testaments." He continued: "This, then, makes the Bible the answer to your question about a book affecting my life. I don't mean to pose as a Bible student, and perhaps it is only now in the last few years that I've recognized its effect on me."

DUTCH PAYS HIS WAY

With savings from his summer jobs, a Needy Student Scholarship, and another job at school, Dutch was able to scrape together enough money to attend Eureka College. At almost six feet tall and 175 pounds, he was a strapping seventeen-year-old when he began his freshman year in 1928, tackling a full load of courses that included rhetoric (the study of the effective use of language), French, history, English literature, and math. Reagan later said, "Eureka was everything I had dreamed it would be and more," and would go on to write about the advantages of small colleges in general: "As in a small town, you couldn't remain anonymous at a small college. Everybody was needed. . . . [T]here's a job for everyone, and everybody gets a chance to shine at something and build their sense of self-confidence. You get to discover things about yourself that you might never learn if you were lost in the crowd of a larger school."

As in high school, Dutch was also involved in numerous activities: football, swimming, track, student senate, basketball cheerleader, president of the Eureka Boosters club, and yearbook editor. "I've been accused of majoring in extracurricular activities at Eureka. Technically, that wasn't true. My major was economics. But it is true I thrived on school activities," Reagan admits in his autobiography. Journalist Frank van der Linden, who began researching President Reagan in 1975, writes this about his college days: "He studied enough to keep at least the 'C' average required to remain eligible for his extracurricular activities." As a senior, he served as student body president and captain and coach of the swim team. Van der Linden also notes, "He was a quick study, then as now, and could absorb a textbook as easily as he could later memorize lines for his roles in motion pictures." Dutch studied sociology as well but chose economics as a major because, as he said, "one way or another, I'd end up dealing with dollars," and he felt he had received a solid liberal arts education at Eureka.

Dutch began his ascent as a popular student body figure when he gave a speech his freshman year and led a student strike to protest the college's decision to lay off teachers as the economy soured with the approaching Depression. It was his first taste of politics. Of this experience, he declares, "Giving that speech—my first—was as exciting as any I ever gave. For the first time in my life, I felt my words reach out and grab an audience, and it was exhilarating."

A PROVIDENTIAL STORM

Dutch didn't get to play much football his first season at Eureka, and he was convinced the coach didn't like him. He was evaluating whether or not to return the next year when, as he put it, "one of those series of small events began that make you wonder about God's plan."

A high school friend was quitting his job working for a surveyor and suggested Dutch apply for the job, aware that he was struggling to pay for his college tuition. The surveyor hired Dutch and gave him "an offer that was too good to refuse." The surveyor had lettered on the crew team at the University of Wisconsin and had earlier noticed Dutch rowing at Lowell Park. He offered to help Dutch get an athletic scholarship to the University of Wisconsin for the crew team if Dutch worked a year for him. Dutch agreed and decided to drop out of Eureka, save some money, and then go to the University of Wisconsin the following year.

But Dutch's plans were drastically changed, and he would eventually recognize God's handiwork in the redirection. On the day he was scheduled to begin working for the surveyor, Dutch woke up to a big rainstorm and couldn't report to work, so he called Margaret to talk to her before she returned to college for the new school year. Her family invited him to join them on their ride to Eureka, so, having nothing else to do for the day, Dutch joined them. Once he was back at Eureka, Dutch saw his close friends and the school again and found it too difficult to think about leaving Eureka for a strange college in Wisconsin. But he still didn't have enough money for the next year's tuition. His football coach was disappointed to learn he couldn't return, so he helped Dutch renew his Needy Student Scholarship, which had provisions that deferred the balance of his tuition until after he graduated. In addition, the coach arranged for him to get, as Reagan puts it, "one of the more pleasant jobs available to a male at Eureka, washing dishes at Lyda's Wood, the girls' dormitory." Reflecting back, he says, "There it was, all of a sudden I was back at Eureka again."

Dutch called his mother to let her know he was staying at Eureka and to ask her to send him his belongings and learned that his brother Neil had decided to enroll in college too. Moon had a change of heart and, after having worked for three years at the cement factory, liked the idea of college very much. Dutch talked to the football coach about Moon's great athletic abilities and soon the coach had arranged for him to attend Eureka on a Needy Student Scholarship as well.

So with the help of a bit of bad weather, Dutch and his brother both found themselves enrolled at the college that would shape each of their lives in dramatic ways. Pondering over the providence of God, Reagan writes, "I've often wondered what might have happened to me if it had-n't been raining that day."

THE POWER OF PRAYER

When the stock market crashed in October 1929, Dutch's sophomore year in college, the country went deep into the Depression, and the Reagan family was not spared the effects of the morbid economy. The shoe store where Jack worked was forced to close, and he had trouble finding and keeping jobs. Nelle got a job as a seamstress clerk. The family was forced to move to a small apartment, and so when the boys came home from col-lege, they had to sleep on either a couch or a cot. But even in those dark days, Dutch's optimism would shine through. Years later, Reagan would say about the Depression years, "There was a spirit of warmth and help-fulness and, yes, kindliness abroad in the land that was inspiring to me as we all clung to the belief that, sooner or later, things would get better."

One of the most important ways Dutch was sustained and encouraged through those tough times was through prayer. In *An American Life*, he says that because Nelle's strong religious faith had "rubbed off on me, I have always prayed a lot; in those days, I prayed things would get better for our country, for our family, and for Dixon. I even prayed before football games."

Dutch never neglected to pray before a game and never prayed to win: "[B]ut I prayed no one would be injured, we'd all do our best and have no regrets no matter how the game came out." His coach once asked the team if anyone prayed, and, to his amazement, many of his other, older teammates admitted to praying similar prayers before games. That was a defining moment for Reagan: "That was the last time I was ever reluctant to admit I prayed."

DUTCH LANDS A JOB

Just as in high school where he had been blessed to have an exceptional drama teacher, Dutch was fortunate enough to find a talented English professor with a passion and love for teaching drama. Her name was Ellen Marie Johnson, and she had just been recently hired at Eureka when Dutch started there. "Once again fate intervened—as if God was carrying out His plan with my name on it," Reagan would later recall. Under Johnson's direction, Dutch was cast in many school plays and, as a junior, won a prestigious acting award from Northwestern University. After the contest, the head of the speech department at the university even encouraged him to make acting his career. By his senior year, Dutch knew in his heart he wanted to be an actor but wasn't ready to share his dreams with anyone yet. Upon graduation from college in 1932, he decided to pursue radio sports announcing as a more realistic step towards his ultimate goal of acting, figuring he would at least be in the entertainment industry.

It was at this point in his life that Dutch was given, as he would refer to it, "the best advice I'd ever received." After graduation from college, Dutch was anxious to get a job, but jobs were scarce and difficult to come by in the depths of the Great Depression. Fortunately, because of his life-guard job and the swimming lessons he'd given to children in the community, he had met several of their well-to-do fathers. One of these was an influential businessman who told him that although he could get him a job through his business contacts, it would be better for Dutch to find a job in the profession in which he really wanted to work. When the businessman asked him what that might be, Dutch reluctantly shared with him his desire to be a radio announcer. Reagan thought it would sound ridiculous if he told him his eventual goal was to become an actor.

The businessman told Dutch to rely on his own persistence and character and simply begin knocking on radio station doors, hundreds of them, and tell them he'd take *any* job, as long as he could get into the industry. He also told Dutch not to get discouraged and reminded him that a salesman often has to knock on hundreds of doors before he makes a sale—he told Dutch to keep trying no matter how long it took.

Encouraged by this advice, Dutch said his goodbyes to Margaret, who was soon going off to a new teaching job in another town, and headed to Chicago in search of a job. There, because of his lack of experience, Dutch faced rejection after rejection and eventually hitchhiked back to Dixon in the pouring rain, broke and discouraged and desperate to find work.

Upon his arrival home, his father greeted him with the good news of a job opening at the new Montgomery Ward store in town. Dutch was excited because he knew he could move up into higher positions in the company if he did well. After applying for the job, he eagerly waited to hear from the manager. His hopes were dashed, though, when he found out the job had gone to someone else. Later, Reagan would see that painful rejection from Montgomery Ward as another example of the hand of God working in his life.

On the first page of *An American Life,* President Reagan begins, "If I'd gotten the job I wanted at Montgomery Ward, I suppose I would never have left Illinois." He continues, "I've often wondered at how lives are shaped by what seem like small and inconsequential events, how an apparently random turn in the road can lead you a long way from where you intended to go—and a long way from wherever you expected to go. For me, the first of these turns occurred in the summer of 1932, in the abyss of the Depression." He sees this rejection as one of those "seemingly random twists of fate" that are "all a part of His plan." Theologian R.C. Sproul writes in *The Invisible Hand*, "[T]here is no 'what if' in God. He is a God whose providence is in the details."

Losing the Montgomery Ward job, Dutch went looking for work again. Reflecting back, Reagan notes, "Although I didn't know it then, I was beginning a journey that would take me a long way from Dixon and fulfill all my dreams and then some. . . . My mother, as usual, was right."

Jack Reagan was a practical man who believed without question the news reports that told people to stay in their own communities to look for work because very few jobs existed elsewhere. Jack knew from personal experience how difficult it was to look for a job and shared his concerns with his sons. But Dutch had a goal, and he wasn't going to be deterred. In his autobiography, President Reagan says of his father, "He was a proud, ambitious man whose dreams had been crushed by the Depression and I think he understood the fire that was burning inside me—a drive to make something of myself—that had always burned inside him." His father let him borrow the family car, and Dutch continued his quest, knocking on door after door looking for a job as a radio announcer.

His persistence eventually paid off. Dutch landed a job as a sports announcer at WOC in Davenport, Iowa, and met an unforgettable Scotsman named Peter MacArthur who was program director at the station. Dutch had never mentioned he was interested in sports at his previous interviews, but fortunately, this time, he tried a different approach. "This man gave me probably the most unusual audition that has ever been given," Reagan later wrote in a letter. "He put me in the studio all by myself. I was to imagine a football game, broadcast it, and try to make him see it. Well, that is what I did—for about fifteen minutes." Reagan raided his memories and colorfully described one of the games he played at Eureka in great detail. After the audition, the Scotsman "walked back into the studio and told me to be there on the following

Saturday—I was broadcasting a Big Ten game, the Iowa-Minnesota homecoming game."

"And that was the start of everything that has happened since," declared Reagan years later when writing a letter about the best advice he'd ever received. "But the advice that led to that was the thing—that it isn't necessary to have pull, or to have someone get you a position. If you really have faith, and will decide what it is you want to do, and then go out and knock on enough doors, you will find someone willing to gamble on even the most inexperienced person, as I was."

Dutch worked the rest of the football season broadcasting Big Ten games and loving it. It was a dream come true for him. However, even though he prayed for a permanent job, Dutch was told at the season's end that there weren't any openings, and he was let go.

A REGISTERED DEMOCRAT

At twenty-one, Dutch registered to vote as a Democrat, following his father's lead. This may seem surprising at first, but Reagan spoke admiringly of President Franklin Delano Roosevelt. In fact, his description of Roosevelt and his brilliant prowess for handling national crises in *An American Life* is strikingly similar to many people's respect and admiration for Reagan's own term and ability in the Oval Office. Reagan says of Roosevelt: "During his Fireside Chats, his strong, gentle, confident voice resonated across the nation with an eloquence that brought comfort and resilience to a nation caught up in a storm and reassured us that we could lick any problem." It's clear that Reagan fashioned his own demeanor after the strong, confident example of Roosevelt, and no doubt learned much from him about how a president should act when talking to the nation in difficult times.

In later years, of course, Reagan's political views would change dramatically, and he became increasingly critical of the welfare state that had started slowly under Roosevelt and has become a permanent fixture in American life. President Reagan says he once spoke to Roosevelt's son who told him that his father's Depression-era welfare programs were just supposed to be temporary emergency measures rather than "a permanent welfare state."

ON THE AIRWAVES

Dutch was out of work the Christmas of 1932 and over New Year's, but in February, after a staff announcer abruptly quit, he was offered a job at WOC, which he quickly accepted. The new job gave him confidence and enough money to help out his brother Moon who was planning to leave college because of financial strain. Nelle had taught Dutch to contribute ten percent of his income to the church, so he asked his minister, "Do you think the Lord would consider it a tithe if I sent Moon ten dollars a month instead of putting it in the collections plate?" The wise and kind minister told him he thought "that would be fine with the Lord." So Dutch would share his new regular salary, sending Moon ten dollars a month and giving a dime each morning to the first person who asked for a cup of coffee on his way to the radio studio, as well as paying off his college loan. Dutch was careful with his money. He always had a budget, avoided credit, and only spent money he had saved.

President Reagan would refer to the four years at station WOC (which eventually merged with station WHO in Des Moines) as "among the most pleasant of my life." The broadcast made his voice and name well known in the Midwest, and between the radio station and outside speaking engagements, he was soon making a good income. He was even able to help his mom and dad who were suffering financially. His father had been having heart problems, which left him unable to work.

During this exciting time, Dutch developed a wide circle of friends who would keep in touch throughout the years and would later visit him in Hollywood. The staffers at the radio station were impressed by Dutch's lack of arrogance and spiritual strength. A fellow worker said of him, "I always thought he was a deeply religious man. Not the kind who went to

Ronald Reagan enjoyed being a WHO radio announcer in Des Moines, Iowa, from 1934 to 1937. (Courtesy of the Ronald Reagan Library)

church every Sunday. A man with a strong inner faith. Whatever he accomplished was God's will—God gave it to him and God could take it away."

This time of his life, however, was also tinged with sadness. He and Margaret had grown apart since they both had found jobs in different cities. One day in the mail, Dutch received his fraternity pin and the engagement ring he had given Margaret soon after graduation. She had fallen in love with someone else. As Dutch grieved over the loss of Margaret, Nelle reminded him of her "old dictum that everything works out for the best and that every reverse in life carries the seeds of something better in the future." Dutch was shattered by Margaret's decision, but what bothered him the most was that, according to Reagan, "I no longer had anyone to love."

In time, the pain eased, and Dutch began to admit his mother was right. He was a successful young man, still in his mid-twenties, who had achieved his goal of becoming a sports announcer and subsequently gained fame in the Midwest, and now he was ready to begin a new adventure in his God-directed journey through life.

We can rekindle the spirit of America, because God intended this land to be free; because we are free to dream, to plan, and to make our dreams come true.

—RONALD REAGAN, 1980

The American dream is that every man must be free to become whatever God intends he should become.

—RONALD REAGAN, 1971

CHAPTER 5

THE AMERICAN DREAM

*For it is God who works in you both to
will and to do for His good pleasure.*

PHILIPPIANS 2:13

Adam Smith once called Providence "the invisible hand of God,"
an apt description of the miraculous presence and force that
guided Reagan through his early years and shaped him into a young man
of immeasurable character and integrity. But God's divine direction is
seldom more evident in Reagan's life than in the fortunate happen-
stances and events that led him to Hollywood and transformed him into
a worldwide film star.

By the time Dutch was twenty-six years old, he had been working at
WHO radio station in Des Moines, Iowa, for four years. He still wanted
to move up to a larger radio station, which was unlikely since the
Depression was continuing to make it nearly impossible to find a good

job. But this didn't stop Dutch from making new opportunities for himself at WHO.

In the winter of 1935, Dutch convinced the radio station owner to give him an all-expense-paid trip to warm and sunny Southern California to attend spring training with the Chicago Cubs and Chicago White Sox baseball teams. In those days, information on sports games was sent in by wire to the radio station, and the announcer had to add the "color" when describing the action. Dutch convinced the WHO management that if he were actually at some of the spring training games, his on-air play-by-play coverage of the team in season would be much more colorful. He would have to give up his yearly vacation, but he would also be able to miss part of the long, cold, miserable Iowa winter—a fair trade by any measure.

But what was more significant, more enticing about this possibility was that Dutch would be near Hollywood. In 1935, there was only one place an aspiring actor could make it in the film world, and that was Hollywood. Whether this strategy was planned by Reagan or a higher power alone, this trip to California would prove to be another step toward achieving his dreams and ultimate life purpose.

GOD'S HOLDING PATTERN

Sometimes it seems in life that our lives are put in a holding pattern, like an airplane circling to land. We go round and round, waiting for the right moment to touch down at our desired destination. It's easy to become frustrated and impatient in these times, unaware that the control tower and ground crew are doing everything they can to clear the way for us—perhaps, they're deicing the runway or waiting for a storm to pass or orchestrating the takeoffs and landings of other planes. To us, it seems like a waste of time. To the one in control, it's an absolute necessity to keep us safe and everything on schedule.

For Dutch, working at WHO for four years must have seemed like an interminable holding pattern. He wasn't getting anywhere, just circling around, waiting for his big break. But God was no doubt clearing his path, making way for his safe arrival in what would be one of the most historic landings—as actor and president—this country has ever known.

That's not to say that his time at WHO was wasted. Those years in Iowa were fun years, and many lifelong friendships began there. He also learned many useful communication skills, including how to think on his feet, clearly articulate himself, and use his voice and words to paint dramatic images in the minds of his listeners. That was one of the reasons Reagan loved radio: people had to use their imaginations. These verbal skills would all come in handy later in his other careers: as an actor, a spokesman at General Electric, governor of California, and especially as president.

TIME TO LAND

One of WHO radio's featured programs was a famous barn dance presentation, a colorful, dramatic event that had a strong effect on Dutch. He once said, in reference to the influence this program had on him, "[I]t had been a long time since the acting bug had stirred within me, but when it did it came out like a butterfly from a cocoon." Shortly before Dutch's trip to California in 1937, Gene Autry hired an act from the dance program to be featured in one of his cowboy movies. "This suddenly made acting and movies seem very close," Reagan later stated. "By strange coincidence, at just about this time, a theater owner in Des Moines called me, and asked if I had ever thought of taking a screen test. I thought he must be a mind reader . . . it just added to the restlessness and the sudden realization that sports might not be the only course my life would follow."

Dutch knew that the probability of his getting into movies was slim. He writes in his autobiography, "Every week, there were hundreds of young people . . . who stepped off a train at Union Station in Los Angeles who had exactly the same dream that I did, and they got no closer to realizing it than a studio front gate."

But once he was in California, he could think of nothing else. His passion for his broadcasting waned, and what he felt instead was a conviction—the prompting of the Holy Spirit, perhaps—but a conviction to take the next big step toward fulfilling his destiny. "Some of Nelle's fey [visionary] quality regarding hunches rubbed off on me," Reagan attests. "There have been a few moments in my life when I have known, or at least had a positive feeling, that something would happen. . . . [S]omewhere within myself was the knowledge I would no longer be a sports announcer."

Upon his arrival in Los Angeles, Dutch was met by a terrible storm with torrential rain, high winds, and flooding. He had planned to take a boat to Catalina Island that evening, but no boats or seaplanes were allowed out due to the hazardous conditions caused by the great squall. So, instead, he looked up an old friend from Iowa, and they went out to dinner. This friend, by coincidence, had landed some small parts in pictures. Everything was falling into place for Dutch and his revived dream and desire. Over dinner, he shared with his friend the recent events in his life and told her that "sports announcing had actually been chosen years before as a steppingstone to acting." She arranged for him to see an agent but advised him not to show up with his glasses on. (Reagan had been wearing glasses since he discovered by accident how impaired his vision was. When just thirteen or fourteen, he tried on his mother's glasses and was amazed how much they helped his eyesight. As Reagan would later describe this discovery, "a new world suddenly opened up to me.")

The next morning at ten o'clock, a practically blind Dutch met with the movie agent. (It should be noted that Reagan did get contact lenses shortly thereafter and was, in fact, one of the first actors to wear them.) The agent immediately telephoned over to a casting director at Warner Brothers and said, "Max, I have another Robert Taylor sitting in my office." Taylor was the biggest name in movies at the time, and the next thing he knew, Dutch had an appointment at Warner Brothers and a screen test. On his first day back in Iowa, he received a telegram offering him a seven-year contract at two hundred dollars a week beginning on June 1, 1937.

"One of my happiest moments, of course, was calling home and telling Nelle and Jack what happened," Reagan writes. "[M]y color could only be painted in a light rosy glow. I would don my shining armour and journey to Hollywood."

When Reagan arrived in Hollywood he was filled with awe and starstruck, working with the same people he had grown up watching in his neighborhood movie theater. He never did get over that feeling. In 1971, he wrote in a letter that what he thought was lacking then in Hollywood was the "warmth and generosity of those great stars of yesterday—their willingness to accept and include newcomers like me—where the great helped the less great" and "there was pride in craftsmanship."

A horrible thunderstorm had again changed the course of Reagan's life. It led him to call an old friend which led to an audition which led to a decades-long movie career. During his career as an actor, he performed in fifty-three feature length films. And that was just the first mark of his powerful impact on the world. Reagan's plane had definitely landed, and it would take off again many times in his life to greater and greater heights.

In Hollywood, Reagan quickly gained a reputation at the studios for being a dependable guy. He was never late, never hung-over, and always a pleasure to work with. In fact, he was soon dubbed "One-Take-Ronnie" because he was always prepared, his lines were always memorized, when it was time to shoot a scene. Longtime friend Mike Deaver says of him, "He practiced extra hard not only because of the competitive beast that lurked inside, but also because he had been taught the value of self-discipline, mostly by his mother Nelle." Attorney General Ed Meese, who also worked with Reagan many years in California and in the White House, concurs with Deaver in his book, *With Reagan*: "Reagan himself was a highly organized and disciplined person underneath his relaxed and genial manner. This also reflected his actor's training—intensive preparation followed by natural delivery." Meese noticed how thoroughly Reagan would prepare for political or social events and knew how to prioritize and concentrate on things he knew were important. "He was a quick study," says Meese. "[Reagan was] able to focus intently on things and to absorb information rapidly." And, as Meese attests, Reagan had a remarkable retentive memory and could recall things he had read years before to make a current point—a skill that would frequently throw off his detractors.

Reagan's first movie was entitled *Love Is in the Air*. The name on the marquee read "Ronald Reagan"—studio executives thought it sounded better than Ronnie or Dutch. When Nelle saw it at a theater in Des Moines, she proudly declared to a reporter, "That's my boy. That's my Dutch! He's just as natural as can be. He's no Robert Taylor. He's himself."

HIS PARENTS JOIN HIM

Each week Reagan would send a check home to his parents. He also began saving money for them to come join him in California. In October 1937, he wrote, "I'm bringing my parents, Mr. and Mrs. John Edward Reagan, out from the old family home in Dixon, IL., now that it looks like I've got a permanent job—for at least six months more—and for the first time in several years I'm going to get my feet under the table and enjoy food just like mother used to make. And, am I happy!"

In 1938, he sent his parents train tickets. Nelle was, at first, torn about having to move away from her friends in the True Blue Bible Class. But Reagan told her that he needed them in Hollywood, and so they agreed to move. He settled them into an apartment near his, and soon after Nelle arrived in California, she became an active member of the Hollywood-Beverly Christian Church. As she had been in Illinois, Nelle was involved in a variety of volunteer work: doing missions work at church, conducting prison outreaches, and helping alcoholics in downtown Los Angeles and at the Olive View Tuberculosis Sanitarium. Nelle's charity knew no bounds.

Decades after her death, in 1993, President Reagan would make a visit to Olive View, now connected with the UCLA Medical Center, and unveil his mother's portrait, where it would be displayed in honor of her volunteer work. Colleen Reagan was there beside her husband Michael and would later tell me, "It was a very special day for [President Reagan]. You could tell how much his mother meant to him." Reagan told those assembled to honor his mother's memory, "Nelle always said that you didn't wring your hands, you rolled up your sleeves. That's just what she did here at Olive View. This spirit is the backbone of our country . . . Americans helping each other by reaching out and finding solutions . . . solutions that governments and huge institutions cannot fund. I suspect that she is looking down and her heart is touched to know that her work continues."

Nelle Reagan's kindness, generosity, and good character created a ripple effect that cannot be measured, helping many more people than just those she personally aided. She made a positive difference in her son's life, and his life would undoubtedly and powerfully impact millions of others. Studies have shown that during Reagan's presidency the rate of volunteerism and charitable giving went up significantly. Soon after taking office, Reagan created the White House Office of Private Sector Initiatives with the objective to "revitalize the great American spirit of neighbor helping neighbor." In *An American Life*, Reagan expresses his hope that one thing the eighties will be remembered for is "a resurgence of the American spirit of generosity that touched off an unprecedented outpouring of good deeds." His mother taught him well.

REAGAN AND HIS FATHER

Although Reagan had not been as faithful a churchgoer while living in Des Moines, Nelle's influence had a strong effect on him in California, and he started attending church with her on a regular basis again. Much of his behavior was altered, in fact, upon his parents' arrival, now that he had more than just himself to worry about. Reagan was supporting two households, so he didn't spend money on self-indulgences and enjoyed simple, inexpensive activities like going to the beach or playing cards with his old friends. He continued to read voraciously, as he did his entire life, and stayed in close contact with his parents, phoning and visiting them regularly. It became a Sunday night tradition for Reagan to take his parents out to a restaurant for Jack's favorite meal, spaghetti and meatballs.

Out of love for his father and concern for his poor health, Reagan created a job for Jack as his personal assistant, handling his scads of fan mail. Maureen Reagan recalls, "My grandfather was too proud to take a handout, and this was Dad's way of seeing that his father had what he needed while he held fast to one of the things he needed most: his pride." She writes, "Jack had had several heart attacks by this time, the residual effects of a lifelong drinking problem." He was also a three-pack-a-day cigarette smoker, which would have certainly contributed to his heart problems.

Reagan said that one day his father brought him a letter from a young woman who had written asking for a photo of him before she died. Ronald Reagan was skeptical, believing her story was just a ruse to get an autographed photo, but he signed it at Jack's insistence. About ten days later, Reagan received a letter from a nurse saying the photo had made the young lady very happy, and she died with his picture in her hands. Upon recalling this touching story, Reagan added that his father never said, "I told you so."

Reagan started out his acting career appearing in "B" pictures, but that all changed when he played the role of George Gipp in *Knute Rockne, All American*. Portraying Notre Dame football star George Gipp was a dream come true for Ronald Reagan. He was fascinated with the famous athlete and his even more famous coach, the immortal Knute Rockne. In fact, it was from this movie that Reagan got his nickname,

"Gipper," in reference to the line, "Let's win one for the Gipper." The movie would prove to be a big success and Reagan became a big name in the business—and was soon being cast in "A" films. Shortly after the film's release, Reagan's prosperity multiplied, and he bought his parents the first home they ever owned, a Spanish-style stucco house at the border of Beverly Hills and Los Angeles.

Being the quintessential Irishman, Jack loved Norte Dame and the "Fighting Irish." One day, Nelle approached her son and told him how much it would mean to Jack if he could accompany Reagan to the premiere of the Knute Rockne movie, which was being held at the University of Notre Dame. Reagan did take his dad, as well as the star of the movie, actor Pat O'Brien, and the two Irish gentlemen hit it off immediately. Jack also sat next to Notre Dame's Mother Superior at a lunch during the weekend festivities—an encounter that made Ronald Reagan more than a little nervous. Much to his surprise though, the Mother Superior enjoyed Jack's company tremendously and told Reagan after lunch that his father was the most charming man she had ever met.

After returning home, Jack told Nelle and Neil that he had "the most wonderful time of his life" at the Notre Dame premiere and didn't care if he never took another breath. Jack's health had been getting steadily worse for some time—no doubt the cumulative effects of a life of hard drinking and chain-smoking. But it was while living in California that Jack put an end to his lifelong drinking habit. Gazing out a window one night, he told Nelle he often wondered what their life would have been like if he hadn't had the drinking problem and then threw out a big jug of wine he had hidden from her. He never drank again. Jack even started attending church, regularly visiting the Catholic church near their house. Soon after his trip to Notre Dame, however, Jack's hard living caught up to him, and he died. Shortly after his death, Nelle shared with her son how much the trip to Notre Dame meant to Jack. "I was there," Jack had told Nelle, "when our son became a star."

In 1981, when Reagan was president, he gave a Father's Day Proclamation in which he paid homage to fathers, undoubtedly thinking of his own: "Our fathers bear an awesome responsibility—one that they shoulder willingly and fulfill with a love that asks no recompense. By turns both gentle and firm, our fathers guide us along the path from infancy to adulthood. We embody their joy, pain, and sacrifice, and inherit memories more cherished than any possession.

"On Father's Day each year, we express formally a love and gratitude whose roots go deeper than conscious memory can recite. It is only fitting that we have this special day to pay tribute to those men—who deserve our deepest respect and devotion. It is equally fitting, as we recall the ancient and loving command to honor our fathers, that we resolve to do so by becoming ourselves parents and citizens who are worthy of honor."

THE WOMEN IN HIS LIFE

Ronald Reagan's relationship with his parents had a great deal of influence on his later interaction with other people, personally and professionally. From his father, he learned to be understanding and unprejudiced. But, without question, his greatest influence was his mother, and her impact can be clearly seen in his kind, loving treatment of women.

Because of his mother's shining example, Reagan had a high esteem for women; he was impressed with what they were capable of and respected and admired them immensely. Michael John Sullivan, author of *Presidential Passions*, says of him, "Women were valued individuals, if not exalted human beings, and it appears that Reagan never allowed himself to perceive them simply as sex objects." Reagan's respect for women was perhaps never more clear than his appointment of Sandra Day O'Connor to the United States Supreme Court—thus becoming the first president to put a woman in that esteemed position. In fact, Reagan appointed more women to the cabinet and high government positions than any other president up to that point in American history.

Reagan's respect for women carried over into his personal life as well, and he was a true believer in the power of romantic love. According to Sullivan, "Reagan was a pure romantic—it was good, solid, enduring relationships that Reagan searched for throughout his life." In his book, Sullivan describes the experiences of several beautiful young actresses when they met the twenty-six-year-old Reagan: "Given the loose morality of the occupational environment, pretty actresses were used to having at least some sexual advances toward them by the males they encountered. They were pleased to discover that the newcomer was anxious first to establish a friendship, and only then proceed cautiously on to romance."

While filming the movie *Brother Rat*, a romantic comedy, Reagan met Jane Wyman, and sparks flew. Michael Reagan, Wyman and Reagan's son, writes in his autobiography, "Mom was reportedly smitten with him at first glance." Jane herself would later say, "I was drawn to him at once. He was such a sunny person." Jane was a beautiful and vivacious young movie star just starting out in Hollywood. She had been a dancer for years, but when she began her acting career, directors consistently cast her in comedy roles as a bubbly, perky blonde. Ronald and Jane began dating shortly after filming began, and she was impressed by his vast knowledge, his goodness and kindness to everyone, and especially his devotion to his mother.

Jane had had a difficult childhood, growing up in an extremely strict home with many rules. She called her upbringing "claustrophobic." Her home was certainly not like the loving and supportive environment of the Reagans, and Jane was not close to either of her parents. As she would note, "Ronnie had this wonderful relationship with his mother. I sensed it. I wanted to have a part of it."

After dating for two years, the two became engaged. A month before their wedding, they went along with a group of entertainers on a variety-style road show around the country with famed gossip columnist Louella Parsons. When they stopped in Washington, D.C. for a show, Reagan persuaded Jane and another actress named Joy Hodges to go

Ronald Reagan's first wife, the stunning movie star, Jane Wyman. (Courtesy of Young America's Foundation)

with him out to visit Mt. Vernon, George Washington's home in Virginia. Hodges remembered how eager Reagan was to go there and how fascinated he was with everything at Mt. Vernon. Later in their marriage, Jane had a reproduction of Washington's writing desk, an object of particular interest for Reagan, made and placed in their home.

Reagan's admiration for Washington ran deep—America's first president was also a Christian who believed in God's providence in his own life—and he noted in 1983, while serving as president, "The image of George Washington kneeling in prayer in the snow is one of the most famous in American history. He personified a people who knew it was not enough to depend on their own courage and goodness; they must also seek help from God, their Father and Preserver." Another time, in a speech also in 1983, he observed, "The founding fathers believed that faith in God was the key to our being a good people and America's becoming a great nation. George Washington kissed the Bible at his inauguration. And to those who would have the government separate us from religion, he had these words: 'Reason and experience both forbid us to expect that national morality can prevail in exclusion of religious principle.'"

"Ronnie" and "Janie"—as they referred to each other—were married at the Wee Kirk O'Heather Church on January 26, 1940, with the ceremony conducted by the pastor of the Hollywood-Beverly Christian Church. The stunningly beautiful bride wore a pale blue satin gown and a mink hat with a veil and held a matching elegant mink muff covered with orchids. The handsome groom wore a dark-blue suit with a white handkerchief in his breast pocket in addition to the carnation on his lapel. The attractive pair was called the "ideal Hollywood couple" by the press.

Jane was made to feel right at home in the Reagan family. Jane and Nelle became as mother and daughter, a relationship they both desired, especially since Nelle never had a daughter and Jane was not close to her own mother. Jane attended church with Nelle—Ronald and Jane had joined the Hollywood-Beverly Christian church the May after their marriage—and Jane even taught a Sunday school class, which pleased Nelle immensely.

Life was moving quickly for the newly married couple. Both of their careers continued to thrive, and, on January 4, 1941, Jane gave birth to their first child, Maureen. It was a difficult labor for Jane, but the young couple couldn't have been more thrilled at this new addition to their happy family. Not long after the birth, the Reagans built a lovely eight-room house with a magnificent view of Los Angeles and the Pacific Ocean, which also included the obligatory Hollywood swimming pool.

In *First Father, First Daughter*, Maureen writes of the many good memories of growing up in the Reagan household—including the regular trips to the Brown Derby restaurant. In fact, the Reagans were such a fixture at the famous celebrity hangout that they were called the "first

family of the colony of actors" in the press. Times were good for the bur-
geoning family, Maureen recalls in her book and describes her father's
reading books, telling stories, reciting poems, and singing songs to her
when tucking her into bed at night. One of Maureen's fondest memories
was of her father reciting and acting out the poem, "The Shooting of
Dan McGrew," by Robert Service, a favorite childhood poem of his
about a saloon in the wilds of the Yukon. Years later, when Reagan was
president and having a state dinner with the Queen of England on a trip
abroad, he was seated between the Queen and the Queen Mother.
Reagan and the Queen Mother had a great time together reciting the
eleven-stanza poem from memory.

A JOURNEY HOME AND A JOURNEY AWAY

In September of 1941, Ronald Reagan was sitting next to his mother Nelle
in a private car on a train traveling through the countryside towards
Dixon, Illinois. While other celebrities on the trip were having drinks at
the bar, Reagan and his mother sat together reading the Bible and praying. He still held his Christian beliefs and had been studying the United
States Constitution, which he referred to as "the Bible of democracy."

Reagan had left Dixon as a local hero nine years earlier. Upon his
return he was a nationally known Hollywood movie star. Reagan never
neglected his mother though and, in fact, made a point to include her as
much as possible in his successful life and career. With each accomplishment Reagan would say something like, "Look Ma, it's your son, the
radio announcer," or, "Look Ma, it's your son, the movie star." One reason Reagan was so eager to share his fame and fortune with his mother
is because he clearly recognized she was one of the main reasons he had
achieved his dreams. This was his way of saying "thank you" to her for
all she had done. Nelle would often go to the studio in Hollywood and
quietly and proudly watch her son as he acted on the movie set, where
she was a well-liked guest and always welcome.

Now a successful actor, Ronald Reagan and his mother Nelle were invited to visit boyhood town, Dixon, Illinois, for the annual Petunia Festival, 15 August 1950. (Courtesy of Young America's Foundation)

When the train stopped in Dixon, Reagan was greeted by a group of old friends and neighbors. He modestly exchanged words with them as Nelle stood next to her now-famous son on the station platform enjoying the moment. Jane was disappointed that she had to miss the trip, but she was unable to travel due to recent minor surgery.

Nelle sat next to her movie star son as they rode down the streets of Dixon in a convertible, waving and smiling to the crowd that had gathered. Although the occasion had been proclaimed "Louella Parsons Day" because the famed columnist was also from Dixon, the majority of the street banners read "Welcome Home, Dutch!" The happy onlookers in the crowd were also cheering for Nelle, who had done so much for the citizens of Dixon. Nelle visited with all of her old friends from church, and she would look back on this time, enjoying her son's success and his popularity back in their hometown, as one of the highlights of her life.

Reagan's life was exceeding his dreams. In 1942, he delivered his most acclaimed performance and what, years later, he would describe as

Enjoying a picnic in hometown Dixon, Illinois, with his mother Nelle and friends, 15 August 1950. (Courtesy of Young America's Foundation)

his favorite role in the movie *King's Row*. It was in this picture that he delivered one of his most famous lines, "Where's the rest of me?" which became the title of his 1965 autobiography. In the movie, Reagan's character wakes up from an accident in the railroad yards to discover that both of his legs have been amputated. He looks down at his mangled body and exclaims the harrowing line. Nineteen forty-two would prove to be a banner year for the Reagans, probably the pinnacle of Ronald's movie career.

But while things were booming for the Reagans, America was committing itself to war. When working in Iowa as a sportscaster, Reagan had enlisted as a private in the U.S. Army Reserve and in 1937 was promoted to second lieutenant in the Calvary Reserve Corps at Fort Des Moines. Incidentally, it was while serving in the cavalry that Reagan learned to ride a horse—and thus began a lifelong love of horseback riding. By 1942, the United States was involved in World War II, and Reagan was called to active duty at Fort Mason, California. He had to leave his wife and baby daughter, like so many other men across America. However, because his eyesight was so poor, he failed the eye exam and couldn't go on active duty. Instead, he was transferred to the Army Air Corps and assigned to the 1st Motion Picture Unit in Culver City, California, where Reagan would eventually rise to the rank of captain. This unit made over four hundred training films, which were inspiring and very helpful in training our nation's fighting men for war.

As daughter Maureen Reagan attests, the time Reagan spent serving in the military away from his family and his movie career ended up hurting both considerably. Although Jane had been very successful early on in her career being cast as a "perky blonde," producers were now casting her in sad, tragic roles. Jane lived her characters twenty-four hours a day, and, according to Maureen, her obsession to "become" the unhappy characters she was portraying made it very difficult on others around her—including her children.

THE REAGAN CHILDREN

Michael Reagan likes to say that the reason he became part of the Reagan family was because of his sister Maureen. She wanted a brother so much that she was willing to empty out her piggy bank in order to buy one. So, in March 1945, Jane and Ronald Reagan adopted their son Michael. Years later, President Reagan wrote about his feelings towards his son, "Traveling back in my mind to Michael's babyhood, seeing again his impish, angelic smile and recalling his unlimited energy, I now realize that many adopted children do see themselves as different. . . . But, as a parent then, I didn't know how Michael felt inside. To me, he was my adorable little son, and from the moment he first smiled at me, I never recalled he was adopted."

But life was moving fast for the young stars, Ronald Reagan and Jane Wyman, and time with the children was not always easy to arrange. In her autobiography, Maureen describes how busy her parents were with their careers while she was growing up, and although she doesn't condemn them for this, she does bring attention to what a blessing it was to have her grandmother Nelle in her life: "My father's mother, Nelle, whom I always called Gramsie, filled much of the void left by my parents' careers, she was a constant in our young lives" and "a steadying influence in mine." Starting as early as two years of age, Maureen began attending Sunday school at Nelle's church, where she received a perfect attendance pin, and would stay at Nelle's house every Saturday night. Nelle told Maureen, "Mermie, always remember that your father is a man of principles" and shared with her the story of how her father had resigned from a country club in Los Angeles when he found out they excluded Jews from membership. Michael Reagan would also remember fondly the tremendous, positive influence Nelle was in their young lives. Michael would stay overnight on Saturdays too, go with his grandmother and sister to church in Nelle's old Studebaker, and be brought back for brunch at Nelle's house. "She was the one who instilled a Christian attitude in the entire family," Michael would later say.

Grandparents have always played a tremendous role in the lives of children, often directing their spiritual lives. There is perhaps no greater illustration of the power of their influence than the example of the babushkas and the Russian Revolution. When the Communist government came into power, the ruthless leaders set out to remove God and all religion from public life. They destroyed thousands of churches, synagogues, seminaries, Bibles, and other religious books. In their new society, it was deemed illegal to worship God, and the Communists would go to any lengths to destroy religious faith—from imprisoning people to torturing or killing them. These Communist leaders, however, didn't count on one thing: the babushka, or old grandmother. The Communists assumed these old matriarchs were harmless, and their old traditions and old ways of thinking would soon die off.

However, when the Berlin Wall came down and communism disintegrated, the Communist leaders were shocked to discover that millions of Russians still believed in God and worshipped Him. As hard as they had tried for more than seventy years, the Communists were unable to snuff out religion. Much of the credit for keeping faith alive is due to these babushkas. These quiet old women were the ones who cared for the babies and children, quietly singing hymns to them in their cradles and whispering Scripture and sharing the Gospel of Jesus Christ with their grandchildren. Nelle also knew the importance of this relationship, and she gave her grandchildren Michael and Maureen the foundation for a firm faith.

THE GOOD GUY

On the screen, as well as in real life, Reagan preferred to play roles in which he was the good guy. Almost without exception, he was cast as the nice, clean-cut, all-American man who always did the right thing. And he wouldn't have had it any other way. Of course, in the Golden Era of Hollywood, most movies had noble themes, such as honor, duty, valor, and pride in our national heritage. There was a clear distinction between right and wrong. Jack Warner of Warner Brothers studio (where Reagan was under contract) said all of his movies had to have a moral to the story with a noble hero and an immoral scoundrel, both sharply defined.

Although Reagan would never get to act in as many westerns as he would have liked (at that time actors were under contract with the studios and often were not given the freedom to choose the pictures they would like to do), it was this classic American genre that best captured the ideals he believed in. In a speech in 1984, Reagan would speak about these ideals: "In *Year of Decision*, 1846, Bernard DeVoto explained what drove our ancestors to conquer the West, create a nation, and open up a continent. If you take away the dream, you take away the power of the spirit. If you take away the belief in a greater future, you cannot explain America—that we're a people who believed there was a promised land: we were a people who believed we were chosen by God to create a greater world."

In an article entitled "Rediscovering the Classic Western," Spencer Warren described the western of the forties and fifties as a movie in which there was a fearless man of character and rugged virtue who treated women with respect. This hero was willing to use his gun only when absolutely necessary—to bring about justice and save the community. The characters in the old westerns were those tough men and women who had set out to explore new and beautiful lands at a time when our country was still young. The West had an honor code by which the hero lived. "Are not America's liberty and enormous progress over the past two centuries the fruit of her ideals?" Warren observes.

The classic Hollywood western directed the movie watcher toward towering ideals and truths. This stands in stark contrast to the movies in the sixties and seventies where there were no moral absolutes and the bad guys were often portrayed as likable, sympathetic characters, such as Paul Newman and Robert Redford's charming outlaws in *Butch Cassidy and the Sundance Kid*.

Reagan detested how movies had changed in the sixties and seventies and wrote in a letter while governor, "[T]hose pictures with no four-letter words, no nude scenes, no blatant sex, no vulgarity were better theatre than today's realism." As governor he wrote a letter commending a fellow actor for the way he had closed a show, saying, "I have felt for a long time that the people of our land are hungry for a return to things of the spirit. Not enough of us use our talents and our positions in testimony to God's goodness."

Reagan liked to play the hero in movies and especially loved classic Western movies. He is seen here as Frame Johnson in the movie Law and Order, *1953.* (Courtesy of Universal International Productions)

Aleksandr Herzen, the Russian writer, warned, "To shrink from saying a word in defense of the oppressed is as bad as any crime." Well, I pledge to you that America will stand up, speak out, and defend the values we share. To those who would crush religious freedom, our message is plain: You may jail your believers. You may close their churches, confiscate their Bibles, and harass their rabbis and priests. . . . You may forbid the name of Jesus to pass their lips. But you will never destroy the love of God and freedom that burns in their hearts. They will triumph over you.

—RONALD REAGAN, 1983

We've been blessed with the opportunity to stand for something—for liberty and freedom and fairness. And these things are worth fighting for, worth devoting our lives to.

—RONALD REAGAN, 1985

CHAPTER 6

A ONE-MAN BATTALION NAMED RONALD REAGAN

In You, O Lord, I put my trust; Let me never be ashamed;
Deliver me in Your righteousness. Bow down Your ear to me,
Deliver me speedily. . . . For You are my rock and my fortress;
Therefore, for Your name's sake, Lead me and
guide me. . . . Into Your hand I commit my spirit;
You have redeemed me, O Lord God of truth.

PSALM 31: 1–5

One of Reagan's most monumental contributions as president was his struggle against and ultimate triumph over communism as embodied in the Soviet Empire—and it was a struggle that began while working in Hollywood and would follow him for the next forty years of his life. Reagan's Christian worldview and relationship with God and His son, Jesus Christ, fueled his fight against this ever-growing political threat to liberty. "For the West, for America, the time has come to dare to show to the world that our civilized ideas, our traditions, our values, are not—like the ideology and war machine of totalitarian societies—just a façade of strength," Reagan said in a speech at the University of Notre Dame. "It is time for the world to know our intellectual and spiritual values are rooted in the source of all strength, a belief in a Supreme Being, and law higher than our own."

Speaking at a ceremony in observance of Captive Nations Week in 1983, Reagan said, "Two visions of the world remain locked in dispute. The first believes all men are created equal by a loving God who has blessed us with freedom. Abraham Lincoln spoke for us: 'No man,' he said, 'is good enough to govern another without the other's consent.'

"The second vision believes that religion is opium for the masses. It believes that eternal principles like truth, liberty, and democracy have no meaning beyond the whim of the state. And Lenin spoke for them: 'It is true, that liberty is precious,' he said, 'so precious that it must be rationed.'

"Well, I'll take Lincoln's version over Lenin's, and so will citizens of the world if they're given free choice.... With faith as our guide, we can muster the wisdom and will to protect the deepest treasure of the human spirit—the freedom to build a better life in our time and the promise of life everlasting in his kingdom."

In similar remarks at the Convention of the National Association of Evangelicals, March 8, 1983, Reagan spoke on the morality of the Soviet Union along with a number of other moral issues. This speech became known as the "Evil Empire" speech when he called the Soviet Union an evil empire and said there was a "struggle between right and wrong and good and evil."

Christianity and communism are diametrically opposed to each other in their basic premises. At the center of communism is atheism, a doctrine that denies the existence of God and thereby removes God from our purpose for life. Chuck Colson explains the stark differences between

Christianity and communism in his book, *Kingdoms in Conflict*: "The Christian believes that the dynamic of all history is spiritual, that its unfolding reveals God's dealings with men, that Jesus Christ is God in the flesh, and that at the end of history, He will reign over all the nations. For Marxists, the material realm is all there is. God and the spiritual order are illusions. . . . Communists are materialists and determinists; individuals count for nothing, the collective or state for everything." He goes on to observe that Christianity and communism are also at odds because "each is a religion and each is inherently expansive and evangelistic."

Although Marxists claim their system is scientific, Colson says anyone who has visited Communist countries knows better. Communists have their own "saints" (Marxist philosophers) whom they study with the same reverence Christians give the Bible. Colson says, "May Day marches and other public ceremonies are atheistic liturgies whereby unbelievers worship the superiority of unbelief." Marxism is a religion because it attempts to explain reality and believes one day, after class struggles against capitalism, man will reach utopia in a classless society. Christians and Jews are especially persecuted and killed in these countries because they are the enemy and pose such a threat to communism's world domination.

Ronald Reagan believed strongly that there is intrinsic, God-given dignity and value in each individual. And given that, what could be worse than a people having stripped from them their freedom to know and worship God, their maker and the giver of life?

In 1980, Reagan said the Communist party taught a child "from the beginning of his life that it is a human being whose only importance is its contribution to the state—that they are wards of the state—that they exist only for that purpose, and that there is no God, they are just an accident of nature. The result is they have no respect for human life, for the dignity of an individual. . . . [T]he Communist party has substituted Karl Marx for God."

In the Bible, we find just the opposite of what communism teaches. King David writes these words about God, "For You have formed my

President Reagan looks across the DMZ towards Communist North Korea at Guard Post Collier, South Korea, 13 November 1983. (Courtesy of the Ronald Reagan Library)

inward parts; You have [woven] me in my mother's womb. I will praise You, for I am fearfully and wonderfully made; Marvelous are Your works, And that my soul knows very well. My frame was not hidden from You, When I was made in secret. . . . [Y]our eyes saw my substance, being yet unformed. And in Your book they all were written, The days fashioned for me, when as yet there were none of them." (Psalm 139:13–16)

To understand Ronald Reagan and what compelled him to act in all walks of life—but especially as it pertained to his lifelong fight against communism—you must understand his view and knowledge of God as creator. Reagan truly knew God in a personal way. This is evidenced by both his words and deeds. Reverend Adrian Rogers, then-president of the Southern Baptist Convention, met with Governor Reagan early in the presidential primaries in 1980. Rogers said about Reagan after cross-examining him extensively: "Governor Reagan said that his faith is very personal, that God is real to him. He had a personal experience when he invited Christ into his life. I asked if he knew the Lord Jesus or just knew 'about' him. Reagan replied: 'I *know* him.'"

In his excellent book, *Knowing God*, J.I. Packer says there is a distinct difference between someone who *knows* God and someone who *knows about* God and *knows about* how to live as a Christian. Packer uses the Apostle Paul (speaking in the book of Philippians) as an example of a person who truly knows God: "But what things were gain to me, these have I counted loss for Christ," Paul writes in Philippians 3: 7–10. "But indeed I also count all things loss for the excellence of the knowledge of Christ Jesus my Lord, for whom I have suffered the loss of all things, and count them as rubbish, that I may gain Christ and be found in Him . . . that I may know Him. . . ."

"Those who know God show great energy" and "boldness for God," according to Packer. In the book of Daniel (11:32), we read, ". . . but the people who know their God shall be strong, and carry out great exploits." Packer continues, "This shows us that the action taken by those who know God is the *reaction* to the anti-God trends which they see operating around them. . . . While their God is being defiled or disregarded, they cannot rest; they feel they must do something; the dishonor done to God's name goads them into action. . . . It is simply that those who know their God are sensitive to situations in which God's truth and honor are being directly or tacitly jeopardized, and rather than let the matter go by default will force the issue on men's attention and seek thereby to compel a change of heart about it—even at personal risk."

Packer cites the story of Daniel and his friends in the fiery furnace as a good example of this commitment. He writes, "Once they were convinced that their stand was *right*, and that loyalty to their God required them to take it, then, in Oswald Chamber's phrase, they 'smilingly washed their hands of the consequences.' . . . 'We ought to obey God rather than men,' said the apostles (Acts 5:29). 'Neither count I my life dear unto myself, so that I might finish my course with joy,' said Paul (Acts 20:24). This was precisely the spirit of Daniel, Shadrach, Meshach, and Abednego. It is the spirit of all who know God. They may find the determination of the right course to take agonizingly difficult, but once they are clear on it they embrace it boldly and without hesitation. It does not worry them that others of God's people see the matter differently, and do not stand with them." Daniel, Shadrach, Meshach, and Abednego, says Packer, "were clear as to what they personally had to do, and that was enough for them."

The Word of God tells us, "For it is better, if it is the will of God, to suffer for doing good than for doing evil" (I Peter 3:17), and Paul writes in Romans 8:31, "If God is for us, who can be against us?"

THE REDS IN HOLLYWOOD

When Reagan returned from service in World War II, the dynamics in Hollywood and his relationship with Jane had certainly changed. Jane had been able to continue her career back in the States, and her fame had skyrocketed, while Reagan, who was forced to put his career on hold during the war, came back to a career that was already beginning to falter. Jane was now a superstar, and Reagan, while still receiving steady work, would never again get top billing.

But Reagan's mind was on other matters. For years, Reagan's interest in politics had been steadily growing. He was very concerned with what he saw as dangerous political and cultural changes occurring in postwar Europe, and this interest soon turned into an outright obsession. Later, Reagan would write, "Looking back, I realize that all of these extracurricular activities prevented me from giving full thought to my career." Because of this his film career did begin to falter, but these "extracurricular activities" would shortly become his new mission.

Reagan had noticed since his return that "something new had come into being" in Hollywood. He was referring to the changes he saw in the labor unions in the motion picture business. They had become more violent, more antagonistic, and had developed a strong affiliation with the Communist party. Still, it would take a slow awakening and drastic transformation before Reagan would decide to do anything about it.

When Reagan had first arrived in Hollywood, all contract players were required to join the Screen Actors Guild (SAG). At first, he balked at the idea because he thought it was an infringement of his rights, but later, when older actors told him how they had been exploited in the past, he changed his mind. He notes that he found out how some of the studio bosses were abusing their power, and says, "Throughout my life, I guess there's been one thing that's troubled me more than any other: the abuse of people and the theft of their democratic rights, whether by a totalitarian government, an employer, or anyone else." He credits his father Jack for instilling those beliefs in him.

In the summer of 1941, Reagan was appointed to the Screen Actors Guild's board of directors where he represented the industry's younger contract players. Reagan later said of that time in his life, "I guess I was also beginning a political transformation that was born in an off-screen cauldron of deceit and subversion and a personal journey of discovery that would leave me with a growing distaste for big government. I didn't realize it, but I'd started on a path that was going to lead me a long way from Hollywood." His brother Neil, who was Republican, played a large part in Reagan's change in political views. The two would argue for hours concerning the future of America with Neil complaining about the growth of government and saying that America could not trust their World War II ally, Russia.

Ronald Reagan, however, was focused on and troubled by what he perceived as the rise of fascism in the United States. He joined a number of organizations that were fighting to "save the world" from fascism and began speaking out against the rise of neofascism in America. Reagan tells about a particularly important—in fact, pivotal—encounter that occurred after one of his anti-fascist speeches. "One day after giving one of my speeches to the men's club at the Hollywood Beverly Christian Church where I worshipped, our pastor came up to me and said he agreed with what I'd said about the rise of neofascism. But he said: 'I think your speech would be even better if you also mentioned that if communism ever looked like a threat, you'd be just as opposed to it as you are to fascism.'" Reagan told his minister he "hadn't given much thought to the threat of communism but the suggestion seemed like a good one" and said he most certainly would oppose it if he ever saw it threatening American values.

Shortly afterward, while giving a speech to a local citizen's organization, Reagan again spoke out against the rise of fascism and found a very receptive crowd that applauded with approval. Then he said, "There's another 'ism,' communism, and if I ever find evidence that communism represents a threat to all that we believe in and stand for, I'll speak out just as harshly against communism as I have fascism." His statement was met with dead silence, and Reagan walked off the stage. A few days later, a woman who had been in the audience wrote him saying, "I'm sure you noticed the reaction to your last paragraph when you mentioned communism," and told him she was going to resign from the group because she saw it as a Communist front group. "Thanks to my minister and that lady," says Reagan, as he realized then what was going on in the motion picture business, "I began to wake up to the real world."

So began Reagan's awakening to communism, which led to his stance against it, which ultimately led to his powerful weakening of it through the collapse of the Soviet Empire. And had it not been for that minister who asked Reagan to consider its threat, all of Reagan's immense work might have never been accomplished. That is the awe-inspiring power of Providence. This one man's warning could have been, in its own seemingly small way, the catalyst to the downfall of communism. The Holy Spirit works through people in many remarkable ways, and God can speak to us and through us. "Without God, there is no virtue," Reagan once said, "because there's no prompting of the conscience." Thankfully, this servant of God listened to his conscience and bravely spoke to the young actor—not knowing he would one day be president and have so much influence over the political climate of the world.

It was in response to this prompting, listening to what God was saying and acting on it, that Reagan decided to take a strong stand against communism no matter the consequences. Stepping out to fight communism in Reagan's day was wrought with many dangers and sacrifices, and Reagan has, in fact, said he knows his career in Hollywood was hurt by his anti-Communist stance.

One of the first things that really alarmed Reagan was the growing influence of labor leader Herb Sorrell, head of the Conference of Studio Unions (CSU). According to Reagan biographer Peter Schweizer in *Reagan's War: The Epic Story of His Forty-Year Struggle and Final Triumph over Communism*, Sorrell had been a longtime member of the Communist party who had been trained by Harry Bridges, the head of the International Longshoremen's and Warehousemen's Union. (Soviet documents prove that Bridges was a secret Communist party member who worked closely with Soviet intelligence.) In 1946, Sorrell had called a strike against the movie studios as a power grab to gain total control over all of the labor unions in Hollywood. In fact, according to Schweizer, Sorrell even bragged, "When it ends up, there'll be only one man running labor in Hollywood, and that man will be me."

Reagan was fully aware of the violence and conflict created by Sorrell and his fellow Communist agitators and dupes. "The gates of the studios soon became a bloody battleground of daily clashes between the people who wanted to work and the strikers and outside agitators," remembers Reagan. "Homes and cars were bombed and many people were seriously injured on the picket lines; workers trying to drive into a studio would be surrounded by picketers who'd pull open their car door or roll down a window and yank the worker's arm until they broke it, then say, 'Go on, go to work, see how much you get done today.'"

Reagan discovered many Hollywood liberals just couldn't accept the notion that Moscow had bad intentions, that the Soviets wanted to take over Hollywood and other American industries through subversion, or that Stalin was a murderous gangster. To them, fighting such totalitarianism was "witch hunting" and "red baiting."

One evening during the strike two FBI agents showed up at Reagan's door and wanted to ask him some questions. He invited them in but told them he didn't think he knew any more about the actual extent of

Communist infiltration in Hollywood than they did. One agent responded, "Anybody that the Communists hate as much as they do you must know something that can help us." The agents informed Reagan that during a recent meeting of the American Communist party in Los Angeles, one member asked, "What the [expletive] are we going to do about that [expletive] Reagan?"

The FBI agents confided in Reagan that their investigations had revealed the Communists were attempting not only to gain control of the Hollywood workforce but also—something much more insidious and subversive—to influence the content of movies with the help of several film writers and actors who were party members or party sympathizers. So Reagan agreed to meet with the FBI occasionally to let them know what was going on in Hollywood.

The Communists' strikes and efforts to take over Hollywood organizations had a profound effect on Reagan and made him realize what an impact movies and the media have on public opinion. He later noted, "It was the Communists' attempted takeover of Hollywood and its worldwide weekly audience of more than five hundred million people that led me to accept a nomination to serve as president of the Screen Actors Guild and, indirectly at least, set me on the road that would lead me into politics."

In those unnerving days when the Red Scare was just erupting, often actors and actresses did not know who was or wasn't a Communist or sympathizer. In *Where's the Rest of Me?*, Reagan describes an evening when he found out that the actress Olivia de Havilland was not involved in Communist party work. He told her, "I thought you were one." And she grinned back and said, "I thought you were one. Until tonight, that is." Unfortunately, some innocent actors were unfairly accused of being Communists or sympathizers. Reagan and other actors opposed to communism helped those unfairly accused by urging them to publicly declare their opposition to communism and appear before the FBI and the House Un-American Activities Committee (HUAC).

Along with the violence at the studios and bombings of cars and homes, Reagan had personal threats made against him—scare tactics employed by the Communists to get him to back down from his crusade. One day while doing movie location shots at the beach, Reagan was called to a phone at a nearby gas station. An anonymous voice promised, "There's a group being formed to deal with you. They're going to fix you so you won't ever act again."

At first, Reagan treated the threat as just a joke, but other actors and people at Warner Brothers took it seriously. The police were called in, and Reagan was fitted with a shoulder holster, a loaded gun, and a permit to carry a concealed weapon. Policemen were charged to guard his house. Reagan would later discover that this anonymous group's plan of attack was to throw acid in his face. "I mounted the holstered gun religiously every morning," says Reagan in *Where's the Rest of Me?* "and took it off the last thing at night." He kept thinking to himself, "The very night you take it off may be the night when you need it most."

Reagan was definitely affected by this, terrified that harm would come to him, or worse, his family. The loaded gun rested on the bedside table while the Reagans slept at night. Reagan biographer Anne Edwards writes how Jane remembered waking up, on more than one occasion, to see Reagan holding the gun, sitting up in the bed, having thought he had heard noises in the house.

Reagan would eventually testify before Congress in the House Committee, telling HUAC about Communist activities in Hollywood. The fortitude and courage Reagan displayed in his battle against communism in Hollywood was a shock to people on both sides. In fact, his determination was so great one pro-Communist Hollywood worker went before the House Committee and openly exposed the Communist scheme to take over the motion picture industry. When a congressman asked him what had thwarted their subversive plans, he responded, "We ran into a one-man battalion named Ronnie Reagan." Author and theology professor Dr. Howard Hendricks says, "The size of a person is determined by what it takes to stop him." And Ronald Reagan, with the strength of the Lord, was a seemingly unstoppable force in the fight against communism.

LETTERS FROM A FRIEND

Throughout his life, Ronald Reagan was a prolific writer of letters, and one of his most notable recipients was a lady named Lorraine Wagner. Young America's Foundation, which manages the Reagan Ranch Center in Santa Barbara, California, is a repository of these letters, which Reagan wrote throughout a fifty-year period.

His letter-writing to Wagner began in 1943 when the thirteen-year-old girl saw Reagan in the movie *Brother Rat* and was enthralled by him. She wrote him an enthusiastic letter asking for his autograph and a photo of himself. Much to her delight, Wagner received not only the requested items but also a personal note from him. The two became pen pals and began a friendship that continued from Reagan's Hollywood days, through his governorship, his presidency, and even into his retirement. In total, Reagan wrote 275 letters to Lorraine over the years. His last one was written in 1994. This letter was written in response to a query she had sent him regarding his widely publicized letter to the American people disclosing his Alzheimer's disease. President Reagan's letters to Lorraine Wagner give an invaluable peak into his thoughts and life throughout a half a century.

In a letter dated January 5, 1947, Reagan wrote, "Dear Lorraine: Thanks for the swell Christmas greetings and your earnest best wishes to us, we are happy and pleased at your kindly thoughts for us. May we wish for you a wonderful 1947 every day. . . . We are working every day and if this doesn't make sense you'll know my brain isn't functioning right, too many late strike meeting[s] at night, I think I can sleep standing up." And on January 24, he wrote that he was still working on the movie, *Night into Night*, while Jane was busy on *Magic Town*. He noted that the Hollywood strike was still on along with "many meetings so we don't have much social life."

The letters reinforce how hectic and demanding the Reagan's lives were just after the war. The family also had the added stress, anxiety, and fear from the Communists' threats of violence against Reagan. Jane also wrote a few letters to Lorraine during this troublesome time. In a letter dated March 8, 1947, she told Lorraine that she was expecting another baby and mentioned her movie, *The Yearling*, for which she had received an Oscar nomination. She said, "We are looking forward to the Academy night. I don't know whether or not I shall do another picture before the baby is born. It all depends upon how I feel."

Unfortunately, although Jane had no idea at the time of her writing, these words would prove to be portentous—her childbirth would be a tragic experience and her life with Ronnie was about to face disaster.

I'm still hoping that things will be different when she gets over this nonsense [divorce], so don't listen to things you hear, please. I know she loves me, even though she thinks she doesn't. . . . Keep your fingers crossed for me.

—RONALD REAGAN, 1948

CHAPTER 7

A FAMILY IN CRISIS

The Lord is near to those who have a broken heart,
and saves such as have a contrite spirit.

PSALM 34:18

T wo years after World War II ended, Reagan took an acting role in *That Hagen Girl*, another B-picture that he didn't like or want to do but agreed to as a personal favor for Jack Warner. While shooting one particularly strenuous sequence, which involved Reagan's character rescuing the leading lady, the director made his star dive repeatedly into ice-cold water until he was convinced the scene was perfect. Reagan woke up the following day with a high fever. The combination of exhaustion, lack of sleep, and stress had taken its toll on the actor, and Reagan ended up with a virulent strain of viral pneumonia. He became so violently ill, in fact, he had to be rushed to the hospital by an ambulance. Since the infection was viral and not bacterial, the physicians couldn't treat the illness with antibiotics, and for the first time (but certainly not the last), Reagan found himself fighting for his life. Days and nights of high fevers and chills blurred into one another during that spell in June of 1947. Reagan's breathing was labored and painful, and one night, he later admitted, he was ready to give up and give in to the sickness. But Reagan was being looked after. And that night a mysterious nurse coaxed him breath by breath to keep going.

Little did Reagan know, though, that as he was fighting for his own life in a hospital bed, his wife Jane had been rushed by ambulance to another hospital across town. She was going into early labor. Sadly, their baby Christina was born three months premature and lived for only a few days. Maureen was about six years old at the time and writes, "What I remember most about that terrible time in all our lives was that my parents were kept apart from each other by circumstance. It's funny what a child can pick up, and what I picked up was that my parents were not able to be together when they should be together." After the birth and tragic death of her child, Jane had to return home alone while her husband remained hospitalized.

Reagan's own brush with death profoundly affected him and gave him a greater appreciation for life, as evidenced by his recollection after the ordeal: "The ambulance ride home made quite an impression on me. I couldn't get enough of looking at the world as it went by, and even the most ordinary, everyday things seemed strangely beautiful." For weeks and weeks after he returned home, he was plagued by fatigue and easily became short of breath and clammy with even the smallest exertion. Biographer Anne Edwards notes, "Jane was withdrawn and relations were strained." Reagan spoke to Nelle almost daily, and she visited their house on Sundays. "But," as Edwards writes, "Jane kept more and more to herself. Everyone attributed it to postpartum depression."

In July, shortly after the death of Christina, Jane began preproduction work on *Johnny Belinda*, a movie she had wanted to perform in ever since she had seen the play years before on Broadway. In order to play the character of the sad, tortured deaf girl, Belinda, though, she had to master sign language and lip reading. Jane threw herself into the part completely and concentrated all of her energies into this one performance. Reagan noticed her sudden obsession with the work. Even though he was busy too, finishing up *That Hagen Girl*, which was already behind schedule, and continuing his heavy involvement with SAG activities, Reagan was worried about Jane. When pen pal Lorraine Wagner wondered why she hadn't heard from Jane lately, Reagan wrote back, "Poor Jane, you'd not wonder why you hadn't heard if you could see how hard she's working and boy she's so thin I wish they'd give her rest." Reagan also mused, regarding her work on *Johnny Belinda*, "She started in too soon, I'm afraid, after the premature birth of our baby."

THE DEATH OF A MARRIAGE

By the end of November, six months after the death of baby Christina, Ronald Reagan and Jane Wyman separated for the first time. In her autobiography, Maureen Reagan writes that her father "had the unhappy news of breaking it to me." He started out by gently telling her, "there's something I have to tell you that's not going to be easy for you to hear," and added, "It's not going to be easy for me to say, either." After telling Maureen of the separation, he reassured her that he would always be there for her and said with his voice cracking a little, "Just remember, Mermie, I still love you. I will always love you."

"Dad was floored by what the divorce would do to his relationship with Michael and me," Maureen shares, "He couldn't stand leaving his kids." Reagan took only his desk and books with him to a small apartment—the place where he had lived before he was married. He also took along two items to remind him of his children: a stuffed lamb of Maureen's that he placed on his dresser and an item belonging to Michael.

In December, Reagan spoke hopefully of reconciliation with Jane to gossip columnist Hedda Hopper: "We had a tiff. That's right. But we've had tiffs before, as what couple married eight years hasn't. But I expect, when Jane gets back from New York, we'll get back together all right." Sadly, Jane's return home did not go as he hoped.

Reagan was devastated by Jane's deserting him. Actress Patricia Neal recalled, "My first meeting with [Reagan] took place at a New Year's Eve party in Los Angeles. His wife, Jane Wyman, had just announced their separation, and it was sad because he did not want a divorce. I remember he went outside. An older woman went with him. He cried."

Everything seemed to be falling apart for Reagan, and yet he remained optimistic. In a letter he wrote to friend Lorraine Wagner (dated January 8, 1948), Reagan revealed problems with his film career but still expressed his bright outlook on his personal life: "Thanks for being frank regarding *That Hagen Girl*. I know the reviews couldn't say much for it, and [I] only did it to accommodate Warner Bros. . . . Janie is still a pretty sick girl, in mind, but I'm still hoping that things will be different when she gets over this nonsense, so don't listen to things you hear, please. I know she loves me, even though she thinks she doesn't. . . . Hope the New Year will be a fine one for you and for every one of us. Keep your fingers crossed for me. As always, Ronald."

Reagan was desperately trying to win Jane back. He visited her on movie sets, sent her flowers, and even gave her a poodle. He told the press, "It's a very strange girl I'm married to, but I love her. . . . I know we will end our lives together."

The pair did reconcile a couple of times before Jane finally filed for divorce the next June. In the divorce proceedings, she claimed her husband had become obsessed with politics and the Screen Actors Guild. Her statement ended, "Finally, there was nothing in common between us, nothing to sustain our marriage."

Reagan was devastated by the divorce. Maureen writes, "It just never occurred to him, no matter what their problems were, that he and mother would get a divorce; it was so foreign to his way of thinking, to the way he was brought up. People just didn't get divorced where he came from, in Dixon, Illinois; even in the Hollywood of 1948, people didn't get divorced all that often. Also, he had just told a friend of his that he and mother were getting along really well for the first time in a couple of years, and then all of a sudden mother said, 'Out, now, go, enough,' or whatever, and he didn't know what hit him."

"[A]nd this, I thought, only happened to other people and you read about it in the papers," Reagan himself writes in his autobiography, "I suppose there had been warning signs." But Reagan never saw them. "If only I hadn't been so busy, but small-town boys grow up thinking only other people get divorced. The plain truth was that such a thing was so far from even being imagined by me that I had no resources to call upon."

Reagan was not, as most Hollywood stars are painted to be, a worldly-wise playboy who took marriage and divorce lightly. He was deeply hurt by the whole experience, but he was also aware of who suffered the most. As he writes, "The problem hurt our children most. There is no easy way to break up a home, and I don't think there is any way to ease the bewildered pain of children at such times."

Reflecting on it in their adult years, both Michael and Maureen Reagan believed that the loss of their sister Christina played a key role in their parents' divorce. Michael confides that he didn't think it was a coincidence his parents divorced within a year of Christina's death and notes, "Many families seem to divorce after losing an infant child." Maureen also wonders, "if losing the baby the way they did accelerated some of the problems they were having in their marriage." Michael also revealed (in an interview conducted at the Reagan Ranch in June of 2001) that he thought his mother might have blamed Reagan in some way for not being there when Christina was born and died—even though he was at another hospital fighting for his life. According to Michael, "The loss of Christina hit Mom very hard. Even today, over fifty years later, she still has Christina mentioned in her will."

"It was an interesting period in my life. Nor was it without rewards and sacrifices," Reagan writes in *Where's the Rest of Me?* "By the time it was over, I was president of the Screen Actors Guild—and I had lost my wife."

PRAYING THROUGH THE STORMS OF LIFE

In *When God Doesn't Make Sense*, Dr. James Dobson writes, "And despite what some Christians tell you, being a follower of Jesus Christ is no fool-proof policy against [the] storms of life." Reagan's divorce and Christina's death were certainly storms—times of great turmoil, great pain—but he knew that God would carry him through. "In the world you will have tribulation; but be of good cheer, I have overcome the world," says Jesus in John 16:33. Reagan was fully aware that life would bring him hardships, that all men and women face terrible trials and adversities, but Christ provides a way to overcome them.

Reagan's daughter Patti Davis talks about her father's strong beliefs in God's omniscience and provision. Reagan's words reveal the solid and mature faith he had. Patti writes in *Angels Don't Die*, "When I was about nineteen or twenty, my father and I were in the midst of a conversation about some tragedy that had just occurred—an airplane crash, I think. My father said, 'It's always difficult to think that God has a reason for such things, but that's what faith is about.'" Patti then goes on to note, "My father has chosen, on a daily basis, to try to accept the will of God. He reminded me often that we do have free will. To him, that means a person can choose to trust in God's wisdom, accept it, and learn whatever lessons are being presented at any given moment, or that person can kick and scream and shake his fists at the heavens."

No one is left alone in times of trouble. Christians are given comfort and direction through the living word of Scripture. Reagan understood these truths intimately. In describing the Bible, he once said, "We're blessed to have its words of strength, comfort, and truth. I'm accused of being simplistic at times with some of the problems that confront us. But I've often wondered: Within the covers of that single Book are all the answers to all the problems that face us today, if we'd only look there. . . . The Bible can touch our hearts, order our minds, refresh our souls."

Scriptures offer encouragement for all people, whether those in trouble: "God is our refuge and strength. A very present help in trouble"

(Psalm 46:1); in sorrow: "Blessed are those who mourn, for they shall be comforted" (Matthew 5:4); or simply needing the assurance of an all-powerful provider: "Cast your burden on the Lord, and He shall sustain you" (Psalm 55:22).

In 1922, Helen Lemmel wrote about dealing with such hardships in the song, "Turn Your Eyes upon Jesus."

> O soul, are you weary and troubled?
> No light in the darkness you see?
> There's light for a look at the Savior,
> And life more abundant and free!
> Turn your eyes upon Jesus,
> Look full in His wonderful face,
> And the things of earth will grow strangely dim
> In the light of His glory and grace.

Without these promises, things would have looked exceedingly bleak for Reagan. His daughter, just days old, had died while he fought for his own life, and his wife left him not more than a year after. But Reagan knew of the assurance promised in Psalms 34:18: "The Lord is close to the brokenhearted: He rescues those who are crushed in spirit." There's no doubt Reagan felt God's closeness even—and maybe especially—through his daughter's death and his subsequent divorce. But Reagan must have also felt a distance—after all, even the most ardent believers suffer doubts and despair at times, and Reagan was living through one of the darkest times in his life. He knew also, however, that it is in those direst times when we most need to go to God in prayer.

In the May 1950 edition of *Modern Screen*, Reagan talked about some of his beliefs about prayer and dealing with hardships—just two years after his divorce: "Unfortunately, my rate of prayer increases with my troubles. There hasn't been a serious crisis in my life when I haven't prayed, and when prayer hasn't helped me.

"I remember when my father died about nine years ago. We'd always been very close. He ran a shoe store, but during the last years of his life, he had to give it up because of ill health. Naturally, I was grief-stricken when he died. Yet my faith in some sort of immortality helped me find peace again.

"Even in a minor crisis, faith can help a great deal. When I broke my right thigh during a baseball game, I faced the doctor's verdict without fear. . . . True, I was flat on my back for several months, but I don't regard that as a real misfortune. I don't think God broke my leg, though it's possible that in the pattern of things I was supposed to slow down and do a little reviewing.

"It would be silly to say that those months revolutionized my way of thinking. But when a man is hurt, he can either be very rebellious or else learn patience. I hope I've learned a little patience.

"There was a wonderful line in *Kings Row*—'Some people grow up and some people just grow older.'

"I believe that God intends us all to grow up, and that there are times when all of us ought to take stock and see if we are growing up or if we are merely growing older.

"Sometimes it takes a tragedy to help us grow up. I don't think we can always analyze why things happen, perhaps it's because we don't see all the results immediately. But there will usually come a day when we can understand the purpose behind some misfortunes.

". . . but in spite of all the suffering we see around us every day, I think of the poet who wrote: *God's in His Heaven, All's right with the world*. And I feel within me that this is indeed the truth."

The trials Reagan faced would ultimately give him the strength and endurance to suffer through many more hardships. They would make him more compassionate to other suffering souls. They would embolden him in the face of adversity and fortify his reliance on his heavenly Father. This is the secret glory of all life's tragedies—they test and forge character and give us pause to recognize what is truly important.

"For My thoughts are not your thoughts, nor are your ways My ways," says the Lord in Isaiah 55:8–9. "For as the heavens are higher than the earth, so are My ways higher than your ways, and My thoughts than your thoughts." Remember the metaphor of the holding pattern discussed earlier. While we're in the plane, we're oblivious to all of the traffic control being orchestrated from the tower. That holds true for all of life. We don't know why God directs things the way He does, but we do know He's in control. We may just have to wait for a safe landing in heaven before we're given the whys and wherefores for all that we must endure.

"If the Lord is our light, our strength, and our salvation, whom shall we fear?" asks Reagan in yet another testament to his abiding faith through adversity. "Of whom shall we be afraid? No matter where we live, we have a promise that can make all the difference, a promise from Jesus to soothe our sorrows, heal our hearts, and drive away our fears. He promised there will never be a dark night that does not end. Our

Reagan broke his leg in a charity baseball game and was on bed rest for several months, later using crutches to get around. He is shown here with his mother, Nelle (on the left), and members of his fan club. (Courtesy of Young America's Foundation)

weeping may endure for a night, but joy cometh in the morning. . . . And by dying for us, Jesus showed how far our love should be ready to go: all the way.

"For God so loved the world that he gave his only begotten son, that whosoever believeth in him should not perish but have everlasting life.

"Helping each other, believing in him, we need never be afraid. We will be part of something far more powerful, enduring, and good than all the forces here on earth. We will be a part of paradise."

Soon after becoming president, Reagan gave a speech in which he shared how he had witnessed the presence of the Divine throughout his life and how much he relied on the Lord: "[An] unknown author wrote of a dream and in the dream was walking down the beach beside the Lord. As they walked, above him in the sky was reflected each stage and experience of his life. Reaching the end of the beach, and of his life, he turned back, looked down the beach, and saw the two sets of footprints in the sand. [But] he looked again and realized that every once in a while there was only one set of footprints. And each time there was only one set of footprints, it was when the experience reflected in the sky was one of despair, of desolation, of great trial or grief in his life.

"[So] he turned to the Lord and said, 'You said that if I would walk with you, you would always be beside me and take my hand. Why did you desert me?' And the Lord said, 'My child, I did not leave you. Where you see only one set of footprints, it was there that I carried you.'

"Abraham Lincoln once said, 'I would be the most foolish person on the footstool earth if I believed for one moment that I could perform the duties assigned to me without the help of one who is wiser than all.' I know that in the days to come and the years ahead there are going to be many times when there will only be one set of footprints in my life. If I did not believe that, I could not face the days ahead."

Reagan spoke those words barely seven weeks before the assassination attempt upon his life. Little did he know at the time that he would soon see the Lord lovingly carrying him with His strong arms through the biggest crisis of his life.

I can sum up our marriage in a line I spoke when I played the great pitcher Grover Cleveland Alexander, a line spoken by him in life to his wife, Aimee: "God must think a lot of me to have given me you." I thank Him every day for giving me Nancy.

—RONALD REAGAN, 1990

CHAPTER 8

NANCY GETS
HER MAN

*But for Adam there was not found a helper comparable
to him. And the Lord God caused a deep sleep to fall on
Adam, and he slept; and He took one of his ribs, and
closed up the flesh in its place. Then the rib which the
Lord God had taken from man He made into
a woman, and He brought her to the man.*

GENESIS 2: 20–22

The 1940s was a time of tremendous change for Ronald Reagan. He had started the decade on top of the world: a great family, a successful career, enormous wealth. He ended the decade quite differently—in despair and loneliness. This was the lowest point of his life. His family was torn apart by his divorce from Jane Wyman, and his acting career was beginning a downward spiral. He was not his usual optimistic self. Following his divorce from Jane, he began to re-examine his beliefs and life, and his political beliefs were morphing into something entirely different from his New Deal liberalism.

Early in his acting career, Reagan had been surprised by his own success and assumed his marriage would be just as successful. Now he was a thirty-seven-year-old bachelor, living alone in an apartment, unsure how to get his life back together. A close friend of his once described Reagan as someone who needed to be married. Being single was unnatural for him. In an interview after his divorce, he said, "I was footloose and fancy free, and I guess down underneath, miserable."

Feeling forlorn and lost without his family, Reagan spent most of his time working on films or fulfilling his duties at the Screen Actors Guild. Every morning he would stop by to have breakfast with his mother Nelle. On weekends, he would take Maureen and Michael out to his new ranch. After the divorce, Reagan sold his eight-acre ranch and purchased a larger ranch in Malibu Canyon, further away from the growing city of Los Angeles. Maureen called it "the ranch of my growing-up years."

Maureen fondly remembers the trips to the ranch in her dad's convertible. "Whenever I think back to the period just after the divorce, I picture Michael and me in the backseat of dad's turquoise convertible, happily engaged in some game or story cooked up by our clever dad. Most little kids just hate being on a long car ride, but for us the time would just fly. . . . Dad also mixed in a little history and geography along the way. He'd teach us tidbits of information on the way out to the ranch, and then on the way back he'd quiz us to see what we remembered."

"There were also impromptu lessons in ethics," Maureen reflects about those special times. Stopping once at a small general store, they all went inside and, says Maureen, "Michael and I asked dad if we could have some animal crackers to hold us over until we got home, and he happily consented and paid the man behind the counter for a box of them. Well, after about fifteen miles or so, dad could still hear us munching away at our animal crackers, and he figured the box was lasting longer than it should. As it turned out, Michael and I had thought we were each to get a box, while dad had intended for us to share only one—the one box he had paid for.

"Clearly it was just an example of poor communication, but that didn't change the fact that the owner of the small store had not been paid his ten cents for the second box of animal crackers. And so, without a moment's hesitation, dad turned the car around and went back the fifteen miles to pay the storekeeper the dime we owed him and to apologize for the confusion."

This event obviously made a great impression on young Maureen. After sharing this vignette about her father's honesty and integrity, Maureen sums it up by saying, "That's my father for you."

This story is a powerful reminder of how all of our actions are being watched, especially by our children, and how we need to stick to our principles in both the big and little matters of life—we are all living models to those around us. It's true: actions speak louder than words. Reagan understood this and lived its implications out his whole life.

A COMFORTING HAND

Shortly after his break-up with Jane, Reagan went to England to make a movie. This was an especially low time for him. World War II had recently ended, and the English government was still rationing food. Reagan also had to endure the cold, rainy, and damp English weather. His misery was evident in a letter he wrote to Jack Warner during that time: "I am putting this letter in a bottle and throwing it on the tide with the hope that somehow it may reach you. Perhaps my report of life here in this dismal wilderness will be of help to future expeditions." He then described the hunger and desperation of war-ravaged England and concluded his missive with these words: "My strength is failing now, so I'll hasten to put this in the bottle before I'm tempted to eat the cork."

In her book, *Angels Don't Die*, daughter Patti tells a story her father had related to her as a child that, she says, may explain more about

Ronald Reagan than anything else. "It happened when he was a young actor, working on a film in England," Patti begins. "He was asleep in his hotel room, he said, when he woke up—abruptly, as if something had jolted him out of sleep. He sat up in bed and had the unmistakable feeling that someone was behind him. But when he tried to turn around, he couldn't. Physically, he was unable to move, as though hands were on his shoulders, holding him in place.

"'But suddenly, I didn't want to turn around anymore,' he said. 'I knew that whomever or whatever was behind me was there to protect me. I had the most amazing feeling of peace. I knew I was completely safe, and that I was loved.' 'Was it God?' I used to ask him [and] he would just smile."

Whatever or whoever it was, the presence gave Reagan a sense of peace, comfort, and security—just what he needed in this dark valley of his life.

A WOMAN NAMED NANCY

Twenty-eight-year old Nancy Davis had just recently arrived in Hollywood when she went out with Reagan on a blind date. "When I opened the door to him for our first date," Nancy says, "I knew that he was the man I wanted to marry."

With the help of some family friends, she had auditioned in a screen test with MGM Studios, and was acting in the movie, *East Side, West Side*—during the time in which she met Reagan. While filling out the studio biography with her contract, Nancy wrote that her childhood ambition was "to be an actress," but outside of her career, her greatest ambition was to have a "successful happy marriage."

Nancy's mother was the actress, Edith Luckett. Edith had grown up with her family in a small home in Washington, D.C. While acting in a summer stock in Pittsfield, Massachusetts, Edith met Kenneth Robbins, a young man five years her junior. Ken came from a traditional, respected family in the town, and his parents did not approve of Edith. Ken's father hoped his son would go into real estate and banking, but Ken had other plans. Flexing his independence, he married Edith and moved to New York City, where Edith landed a small role in a play. Robbins tried his hand as a booking agent and a few other jobs in New York but never really made it. So after his father died and left him and his mother a small inheritance, he decided to move home back to be near his widowed mother. Edith did not want to go back with him despite being a few months pregnant.

Anne Frances Robbins, named after both her grandmothers, and dubbed by her mother as Nancy, was born on July 6, 1921. Ken gave Edith an ultimatum, demanding that she choose between returning to Pittsfield with baby Nancy or divorcing him. Edith chose her acting career and found herself in traveling plays dragging Nancy along with her from town to town and from theater to theater. When Nancy was two years old, Edith sent her to live with her sister and brother-in-law in Bethesda, Maryland. The couple had a daughter who was two years older than Nancy, and the two girls later attended Sidwell Friends School, an exclusive school in Washington, D.C. On occasion, Nancy's Aunt Virginia would take Nancy by train to New York to visit her mother and to attend one of her plays. Nancy writes in her memoirs that those six years away from her mother were "a painful period. . . . And I missed her—terribly. No matter how kindly you are treated—and I was treated with great love—your mother is your mother, and nobody else can fill that role in your life." Nancy would see her father and paternal grandmother infrequently over the years but eventually severed all ties with them.

While on tour, Edith met Dr. Loyal Davis, a prominent Chicago neurosurgeon, and the two fell in love and married in 1929. Edith sent for Nancy from Bethesda and, according to Nancy, settled down "into the socially prominent world of Dr. Loyal Davis in Chicago" when Nancy was almost eight years old.

Finally, Nancy had found a stable home, and she would later admit how much of a positive impact both her mother and her mother's new husband had on her: "She had a profound influence on the woman I turned out to be, as did her second husband, Dr. Loyal Davis, whom I have always considered my true father." Nancy truly loved and admired Dr. Davis, describing him as "a man of great integrity who exemplified old-fashioned values . . . a classic self-made man."

The two made a wonderful couple, each complimenting the other's particular gifts and personality. "My mother's world was the theater," Nancy writes in her autobiography. "[S]he was an actress and a real character—fun loving, social, irrepressible, and irresistible. Loyal Davis . . . was serious, dignified, and principled." Dr. Davis was an agnostic, and President Reagan would later share his faith with him. Nancy writes that she once asked him what happiness was, and he answered by saying, "Nancy, it's basically what the Greeks said. Happiness is the pursuit of excellence in all aspects of one's life." As a teen, Nancy encouraged Dr. Davis to adopt her so she could officially become "Nancy Davis."

Edith was also the exact opposite of Nancy's extremely proper and modest Aunt Virginia: "Mother was not only outgoing and gregarious; she was also capable of uttering words that would shock a sailor, and was one of the few women I've ever known who could tell an off-color joke and have it come out funny."

Edith expanded Nancy's social circles tremendously. Since Edith viewed social standing in the community as very important, one of her goals was to move the family up into high society, and she made sure Nancy went to the best schools, wore the right clothes, and, perhaps most important, was introduced to the right people—those who could further her career or position in society. Nancy would later help her own husband in the same way—routinely hosting parties, attending social events, introducing him to many influential people, and encouraging him to use his gifts and talents to run for political office. In fact, Nancy would later say, she learned everything about how to be a dedicated, exuberant wife from her mother, who doted on Dr. Davis constantly and transformed his social life considerably. Edith advised her daughter, "Now Nancy, when you get married, be sure to get up and have breakfast with your husband in the morning. Because if you don't, you can be sure that some other woman who lives around the corner will be perfectly happy to do so."

Nancy acted in a few school plays at Girls' Latin School in Chicago and, after graduating from high school, attended the elite Smith College where she says she majored in "English and drama—and boys." Edith had a wonderful network of friends in theater and show business and was instrumental in helping Nancy get her audition in Hollywood. In 1975, when Smith College was gathering information on alumni, Nancy wrote of her achievements: "I was never really a career woman but [became one] only because I hadn't found the man I wanted to marry. I couldn't sit around and do nothing, so I became an actress."

RONNIE AND NANCY

One day, while reading one of the Hollywood papers, Nancy noticed her name in a list of alleged Communist sympathizers. Shocked and appalled by this false allegation, Nancy went to the Screen Actors Guild President Ronald Reagan to set things straight. Clearing her name, however, was only part of the reason for arranging a meeting with Reagan. By her own admission, Nancy says the overriding motivation for clearing her name was to get the chance to meet Ronald Reagan. She was fully aware that his marriage had recently ended, and so, with the help of an old family friend, director Mervyn LeRoy, she tried to get an appointment with Reagan.

Nancy sat anxiously by the phone waiting for Reagan to call, but he never did. Reagan simply told LeRoy that there were at least three other actresses named Nancy Davis, thus causing the confusion in the press coverage, and that if there was ever any problem the Guild would defend her. This answer didn't satisfy Nancy, though. She writes, "That was reassuring, but it wasn't exactly what I wanted to hear. So I put on a *very* unhappy face." She then told LeRoy, "I'm really worried. I'd feel a lot better if Mr. Reagan explained it to me himself." White House correspondent and biographer, Lou Cannon, writes about Nancy, "When the opportunity to meet him presented itself, she demonstrated an inclination for the main chance that is one of her abiding characteristics." LeRoy eventually called Reagan again on behalf of Nancy, and Reagan agreed to meet her for dinner to discuss the problem.

Nancy's first thought when she opened the door for her date with Reagan was: "This is wonderful. He looks as good in person as he does on the screen!" even though Reagan was using a cane because, to add to all his other troubles, he had broken his leg in a charity baseball game and had just spent eight weeks recuperating. They went to one of the best restaurants in Hollywood, quickly discussed Nancy's media problem, and moved on to other topics. Nancy says, "One of the things I liked about Ronnie right away was that he didn't talk only about himself." She also was immediately enamored with his wonderful sense of humor.

They had a great time that evening and began dating soon after. "I wish I could report that we saw each other exclusively," Nancy writes, "and that we couldn't wait to get married. But Ronnie was in no hurry to make a commitment. He had been burned in his first marriage, and the pain went deep. Although we saw each other regularly, he also dated other women."

Nancy regularly called Edith on the telephone, and the two stayed in close contact throughout her career and love life in Hollywood. Nancy confided in her mother her desire to marry Reagan and her most certain impatience with Ronald's reluctance to pop the question. Nancy would write years later, "I also knew that a divorced man needed time before he was ready to marry again. My mother reminded me that Loyal Davis had been badly burned in his first marriage. He had been terrified of making another mistake, and she had had to wait until he was ready."

But even without the proposal, Nancy and Ronald grew ever closer. "The romance of a couple who have no vices" is how one Hollywood newspaper described their relationship. "Not for them the hot-house atmosphere of nightclubs, the smoky little rooms and the smell of

Scotch. They eat at Dave Chasen's [a casual restaurant], they spend their evenings in the homes of friends, they drive along the coast and look at the sea and a lot of time they're quiet. . . . Nancy knits Reagan argyle socks, though she doesn't cook for him." In fact, Nancy never did take up cooking, and they always had a cook working for them.

Nancy became more hopeful about their relationship when Reagan finally asked her to come to his ranch in Malibu Canyon. She would help at the ranch by painting the fences and later accused him of "marrying me just to get his fences painted." Reagan taught Nancy how to ride horses at his ranch. "I never became a great rider," Nancy writes. "But Ronnie rode, so I did too. I was, I suppose, a woman of the old school: If you wanted to make your life with a man, you took on whatever his interests were and they became your interests, too."

Reagan continued to take his children out to his ranch with him on weekends, but now Nancy joined them. Michael Reagan told me how much he enjoyed those times at the ranch, all of them riding together: "I loved to go to the ranch with Dad on weekends. I remember him picking us up in his station wagon and all of us riding out there. Dad was a great teacher when he taught Maureen and me how to ride a horse. He was always calm and patient, never raising his voice at us. He started teaching us by leading us around the corral on our horse. When he wasn't busy with us, I enjoyed watching him doing his chores: chopping trees and wood, painting fences, training his horses, and other odd jobs around the ranch. Dad was a man's man. I was in total awe of him. I wanted to be just like him."

By now, both Maureen and Michael were attending Chadwick's, a boarding school where Jane had sent Maureen after the divorce and later sent Michael when he was five years old. There Michael would often cry himself to sleep wishing he was home with his mother who was busy making movies. The children were able to go home every other weekend—sometimes their dad took them to Nelle's house to stay overnight, sometimes they went out to the ranch with him.

Another time Michael told me how much he looked forward to

those Saturdays at the ranch "because when Nancy came along she sat in the front seat of the car and I would sit on her lap. I remember her giving me back rubs on those trips. I really liked those back rubs Nancy gave me. Of course I liked to be with my father, but I really looked forward to those rides with all of us in the car and having Nancy's love." Nancy also remembers how much little Michael loved their time together, "I felt sorry for that little boy. He was only three when his parents separated, and he didn't really understand what it all meant. He reminded me of a lost puppy who needed a lot of love and affection."

Although Nancy would occasionally have to interact with Jane when Reagan would bring his new love over to see the children at their house, particularly on holidays, the two women never got along. Nancy writes, "She [Jane] had convinced him that he shouldn't get married again until she did it. It took me a little time, but I managed to unconvince him."

Nancy knew that Reagan's interest in the Guild was a source of irritation in his first marriage and that Jane had publicly said she was bored by all of his talking about politics, and so she made it perfectly clear that she was totally behind his emerging passion. "Even then, Ronnie could see that I was totally supportive of him and that he could trust me," Nancy writes of the time before they were married. "But I loved to listen to him talk, and I let him know it."

At Christmas in 1951, Nancy stayed in Los Angeles to be with Ronnie instead of going to Chicago to be with her family, as she usually did. "I knew Ronnie was the right one for me," Nancy writes. "He was all I had ever wanted in a man, and more, and he was different from anyone I had ever known." After two years of dating, thirty-year-old Nancy was ready for a commitment. Nancy says that at the end of that year Reagan told her "that it wasn't so much that he hungered for someone to love him, but that he really missed having somebody to love." It was then Nancy knew "he had recovered from the trauma of the divorce."

Reporters kept asking them when they were going to get married, and as Nancy would later say, "I was beginning to wonder, too, and I was beginning to get impatient. I knew that I wanted to spend my life with

Ronnie, and time was marching on. I had long conversations about it with my mother, who listened and advised me. We were always very close, and I couldn't really talk about these things too much with my friends. . . . But still, there was no proposal."

Not long afterward, while he and Nancy were having dinner in their usual booth at Chasen's, Reagan said, "I think we ought to get married." Nancy recalls exactly what she felt like when she heard those words: "I was ecstatic. I could have jumped out of my seat and yelled, Whoopee! But I could hardly do it at Chasen's. So I answered calmly, 'I think so, too.'"

They announced their engagement on February 21, 1952. "We were thrilled, and so were our parents," Nancy writes. "But Ronnie still wanted to keep things low-key. We had already agreed on a very small wedding, with absolutely no press. I would have preferred a bigger one, with all our friends, but I understood how Ronnie felt, and if he thought a private ceremony was more appropriate, that was okay with me. By

Newlyweds Ron and Nancy Reagan with friends Bill and Ardis Holden following the Reagans' wedding, 4 March 1952. (Courtesy of the Ronald Reagan Library)

then we felt we were already married, and it was time to make it official."
So on March 4, 1952, the couple were married in a simple ceremony at
the Little Brown Church in the Valley with only William Holden and his
wife Ardis, their two best friends, attending. "The Little Brown Church
was small and out of the way and seemed like a good place to be married quietly," Nancy says. "Ronnie found it; he belonged to the
Hollywood Christian Church, but that was huge and would have
attracted a lot of attention."

The newlyweds drove to the Biltmore Hotel in Phoenix, Arizona, where
Nancy's parents met them for a celebration. "We were so happy on our hon-
eymoon," Nancy writes, "but the first year of our marriage was difficult.
During that year we had our first child, Patti, who was born—go ahead and
count—a bit precipitously but very joyfully, on October 22, 1952."

Meanwhile, Reagan's career was still on a downhill slide. "I thought
I'd married a successful actor," Nancy would write years later, but the
newlyweds were in for some rough years ahead. Reagan was not getting
any scripts to his liking, so he did a couple of movies that turned out to
be unsuccessful. They bought a three-bedroom house in Pacific Palisades,
which at the time was out in the country, but were unable to afford fur-
nishing it for some time. Reagan even turned down several scripts for
$500,000 because he thought they would further hurt his career.

Nancy writes about this difficult time for them in her memoirs, "He
was, as you might expect, pretty low. One evening, when he returned
from a meeting that had evidently been covered by the press, he told me
he had overheard somebody say, 'Well, at last Ronald Reagan is having
his picture taken.' He was crushed, and when he told me about it, I could
have cried for him. I remember going over and putting my arms around
him. How humiliating for a man to hear that!"

Still, even though he endured such terrible moments of humiliation,
Reagan soldiered on with his life, not giving into despair. Just like Nelle
would always say, things will get better. And now, with a strong, supportive wife at his side, Reagan was ready to take on whatever lay in front
of him.

REAGAN GETS A BREAK ON TELEVISION

Reagan was soon offered an opportunity to be the emcee for the Continentals, a famous male singing group who were performing in Las Vegas. Although Reagan had reservations about the job, he took it because he needed the money—he had the mortgage on the new house, child support payments for Maureen and Michael, the ranch, and his new family to support. And besides that, he had little savings. When his career had been going well, he was in the 94 percent tax bracket and only got to keep six dollars out of every hundred dollars he earned.

His move to Las Vegas revealed, incidentally, his lifelong love of books. Ronnie moved into the hotel where he was set to perform, the Last Frontier Hotel, and the owner was overwhelmed with how many books he had packed. Upon seeing them, he said, "I've had a lot of entertainers at this hotel, but I've never seen anyone brings books to Las Vegas." Later, as president, Reagan would write in a letter, "The joy of reading has always been with me. Indeed, I can't think of greater torture than being isolated in a guest room or hotel without something to read."

Nancy felt she really needed to be in Las Vegas with Ronnie to show her support, so like her mom had done with her, Nancy left three-month-old Patti behind to stay with their housekeeper. Nancy sat through every performance for two weeks before the couple finally decided what was already apparent, "The nightclub life was not for us." They moved back to California, and although Nancy had said when she got married that she wanted to give up her career to be a wife and mother, she went back to make two films because finances were so tight. She even starred alongside her husband in the 1957 release *Hellcats of the Navy*.

Television was exciting and new in the early fifties, but Reagan turned down several offers to star in a TV show because, as he puts it, he "was sure a television series could be a professional kiss of death to a movie star." After all, he thought, people wouldn't pay to see a star in a movie theater after seeing them for free on TV. But God had different plans for Reagan, and the hand of Providence again was leading him down a fruitful path, although at the time it seemed to be a step back. Writing in *An American Life*, Reagan says, "In the end, television guest spots not only tided us over financially, but led me to one of those unexpected and unplanned turns in the road—the kind that can take you a long way from where you thought you were going."

Proverbs 21:1 describes how God works in our lives, "The king's heart is in the hand of the Lord, Like the rivers of the water; he turns it wherever he wishes." This passage shows that even the mightiest are at His mercy. And through his work in television, it is evident that a path had been forged for the river of Reagan's life. God continued to lead

Ronald Reagan and General Electric Theater, 1954–62. (Courtesy of the Ronald Reagan Library)

Reagan toward His chief purpose and plan—this humble actor's life was always in the Lord's protective hand.

Not long after his short stint in Las Vegas, Reagan received an offer to serve as the weekly host of and occasional actor in a new show called the *General Electric Theater*, which would feature a new story with a completely different cast of characters each week. Reagan liked the idea because he knew he wouldn't be typecast in a particular role as he would have been on a regular TV series. Reagan was also asked to become a spokesman for GE and would travel the United States visiting the 139 GE plants in thirty-nine states, allowing him to tour the country giving speeches on his favorite topics.

Reagan would walk the assembly lines, shake hands, boost morale, speak, answer questions, and listen to the workers. One time he made fourteen speeches in a day. His talks were first centered on Hollywood, but as he followed the workers' leads, his speeches began to be about the "encroaching government," government's interference in the free enter-prise system and in individuals' lives. In 1990, Reagan described these speeches: "Pretty soon, it [these speeches] became basically a warning to people about the threat of government. . . . I was out there beating the bushes for private enterprise. . . . I'd emphasize that we as Americans should get together and take back the liberties we were losing; with fewer than sixty percent of the voters turning out at many national elections, it was like handing ourselves over to the enemy. Our whole system of government is based on 'We the people,' but if we the people don't pay attention to what's going on, we have no right to bellyache or squawk when things go wrong."

Eventually workers brought their family and friends to hear Reagan's speeches, and he was asked to speak at other local organizations in the towns he visited. His daughter Maureen says, "By the end of the 1950s Ronald Reagan was the second most sought-after public speaker in the country, after President Eisenhower." Representing GE turned out to be an invaluable experience for Ronald Reagan. It improved his speaking abilities and provided him with good, steady work. He observes, "Those GE tours became almost a postgraduate course in political science for me. I was seeing how government really operated and affected people in America, not how it was taught in school."

The GE show ran from 1954 to 1962, and Reagan and Nancy would both later refer to those times as "happy years," even though it kept Reagan on the road much of the time. After the first GE tour, when he was gone for two months straight, Reagan arranged his schedule so he would never be gone more than two weeks at a time. "He was away so much," Nancy shares, "I once figured out that if I added up all his time traveling, it came to almost two years—two years out of the eight he spent working for GE." He and Nancy were able to keep in touch through letters and cards, most of which Nancy has saved to this day. Still, Reagan says, "[T]here were long stretches of my life during that period when my daily routine focused entirely on my family, our ranch, and a horse."

And obviously Reagan did make time and effort to maintain his happy family. Ronnie and Nancy started construction of a new house, and in May of 1958, they had a son together. His name was Ron, but he was known throughout his childhood as Skipper.

SHARING HIS FAITH

In her book, *Angels Don't Die,* Patti Davis focuses on what her father taught her as a child about God and faith, recollecting their lovely conversations together and emphasizing that her father had "embraced the essence of Christ's teachings."

Patti points out that, "The world knows much about Ronald Reagan; it should also be known that he passed along to his daughter a deep, resilient faith that God's love never wavers, and that no matter how harsh life seems, or how cruel the world is, that love is constant, uncon-ditional, and eternal. . . . Ronald Reagan was a father who patiently answered his child's questions about God, and angels, and miracles." Patti explains her father was the one "who talked openly and freely about spiritual matters. I know my mother has her beliefs and her own way of communicating with God, but it's a part of herself that she holds close, which is her right."

"My father taught me to talk to God," Patti continues, "and taught me that prayer is exactly that—a conversation with God." To her many questions, she says, "my father's answers were sweet, simple, and reassuring. He told me that God is about Love; He loves us no matter what we do. We can talk to God even when we're in a bad mood or feeling angry and bitter." Some of her questions concerned angels and miracles, and when she asked her father if Joan of Arc was really visited by spirits, as history suggests, he replied, "Oh, I think so. God speaks to us in different ways. He chose to send angels to her."

These father and daughter talks were not formal lessons but took place naturally while spending time together horseback riding, on walks, flying kites, or tucking her into bed at night. Patti says, "He simply described his own spiritual relationship in such a way that I was left with the impression that God was his friend, and they had deep, unstructured dialogues." He used terms such as "the answer I got was . . ." when referring to his talks with God, and Patti adds, "My father made it seem simple"—his faith appeared effortless.

Reagan used different situations to teach Patti—it's one of the best ways to instruct a child, making good use of teachable moments. Patti says when she was a child they always stopped for ice cream at a shop on their way home from the ranch, and she tells a story about one of their times: "I remember on one Saturday afternoon, the person selling ice cream was very rude to us for no apparent reason. When we got back to the car, my father said, 'You know, you can never know what's going on in another person's life. That woman might have just gotten terrible news, or lost a loved one. Or maybe she's ill. Maybe that's why she was acting like that. You just never know.'" Reagan was always looking for the best in people.

Frequently over the years, Reagan would tell Patti, "God always listens, and He's always watching," and Patti says he let her know, "this is one of the cornerstones of his life. The private man, beneath the public one, has always felt hands on his shoulders, keeping him safe, and he has never doubted that they belong to God."

THEIR DEEP MUTUAL LOVE SUSTAINED THEM

Although circumstances were less than ideal when they married, the Reagans have had a truly magical, romantic, and successful marriage and have worked hard throughout the years to make their love flourish. In December 1951, Reagan wrote a letter to a friend whose husband had recently died, giving her advice and comfort, and said, "Love can grow slowly out of warmth and companionship and none of us should be afraid to seek it." No doubt he was thinking of his own relationship with Nancy, one that had developed gradually despite fears from his first marriage.

Nancy has repeatedly said, "My life didn't really begin until I met Ronnie." And Reagan, when asked by the editor of *Cosmopolitan* magazine to write down "the nicest thing a girl ever did" for him, responded, "The nicest thing a girl ever did for me was when a girl named Nancy married me and brought a warmth and joy to my life that has grown with each passing year." In another interview, Reagan said that coming home to Nancy "was like coming out of the cold into a warm room with a fireplace."

"If our marriage has been successful," Nancy admits, "it's because Ronnie and I have both worked very hard at it. Maybe we tried extra hard because Ronnie had been divorced, and he didn't want to go through *that* again. Both my parents had been divorced, so I too had some idea of what that meant." She also tells about a letter Reagan wrote to her which reads, "[W]e haven't been careless with the treasure that is ours—namely what we are to each other."

As is true with all marriages, each partner has different strengths and weaknesses they bring to the marriage, and often opposites attract

Ronald and Nancy Reagan at the Stork Club in New York City early in their marriage.
(Courtesy of the Ronald Reagan Library)

because we admire the strengths in other people that we see as weaknesses in ourselves. President Reagan explains such complimentary differences between himself and Nancy: "In college I had a philosophy class in which our professors told us that the world was divided into two kinds of people: those who are skeptical of others until the other persons prove themselves, and those who assume that other people are good and decent unless proven otherwise.

"I suppose that pretty well describes one of the differences between Jack and Nelle. And maybe it describes a difference between Nancy and me. I can't say which of us has been right more often than the other. I believe, in general, people are inherently good and expect the best of them. Nancy sees the goodness in people but also has an extra instinct that allows her to see flaws if any are there.

"She's a nest builder and defender of her own. If you've seen a picture of a bear rearing up on its hind legs when its mate or one of its cubs is in danger, you have a pretty good idea of how Nancy responds to someone whom she thinks is trying to hurt or betray one of hers."

Nancy has been a great asset to Reagan throughout his career and has made sacrifices and given encouragement to help her husband reach his full potential. She is an ambitious woman who played a very important part in her husband's ascension to the presidency. Likewise, Reagan has always been very loving and caring towards his wife, just as the Bible instructs husbands to do in Colossians 3:19.

When asked to run for governor, Reagan first said no—he was only interested in helping other candidates. Nancy, however, was in favor of his running and encouraged him to do it, as she would later encourage him to run for president. Reagan was, by nature, shy and introverted and was in a sense a reluctant leader. And perhaps this is what made him a great leader. He wasn't, as Nancy attests, running for president for the power but because he believed he could make a difference. Frank van der Linden writes in *The Real Reagan* that it was after much prayer and meditation that Reagan decided to run for president in 1976. "Nobody in the world could have prayed harder than I did that there would be no need for my candidacy," Reagan said, revealing his reluctance to run against Gerald Ford. "I prayed also that the administration would be successful in solving the domestic and the international problems. Finally, it became apparent to me that Washington wasn't doing what was needed."

Yet, despite her ambition for her husband, Nancy has always been a traditional woman, always pleased to play the role of the devoted wife. "I've always felt that I had the best of both worlds," says Nancy, "a career, followed by a happy marriage." Nancy sees herself as a protector of her husband with a unique, important duty to look out for him and declares one of her roles as wife is to "provide a warm, restful, and welcoming home for my husband. I always did. . . . And I think it made a big difference to him, whether he knew it or not."

And while Nancy may have been the more pragmatic of the two, Reagan was easily the romantic one. He would send letters, notes, a half dozen cards on birthdays, anniversaries, and Valentine's Day. He even sent flowers to her mother on Nancy's birthday just to say thank you. "Ronnie has always been there for me, even during the years when the world was on his shoulders," Nancy attests. "And he takes care of me," she continues, citing small but significant instances of his counting out her vitamins and pills when she would go away for a few days or pulling up the cover on her shoulders at night.

When his son Michael was getting married, Reagan sent him a letter expressing his own thoughts about marriage and gave his son advice, which Michael has worked to implement in his own marriage to his lovely wife Colleen. Michael gave me a copy of the letter. It reads as follows:

"Dear Mike: You've heard all the jokes that have been rousted around by all the 'unhappy marrieds' and cynics. Now, in case no one has suggested it, there is another viewpoint. You have entered into the most meaningful relationship there is in all human life. It can be whatever you decide to make it.

"Some men only feel their masculinity can only be proven if they play out in their own life all the locker room stories, smugly confident that what a wife doesn't know won't hurt her. The truth is, somehow, way down inside, without her ever finding lipstick on the collar or catching a man in the flimsy excuse of where he was till three A.M., a wife does know, and with that knowing, some of the magic of this relationship disappears. There are more men griping about marriage who kicked the whole thing away themselves than there can be wives deserving of blame.

"There is an old law of physics that you can only get out of a thing as much as you put in it. The man who puts into the marriage only half of what he owns will get that out. Sure, there will be moments when you will see someone or think back on an earlier time and you will be challenged to see if you can still make the grade, but let me tell you how great is the challenge of proving your masculinity and charm with one woman for the rest of your life. Any man can find a twerp here and there who will go along with cheating, and it doesn't take all that much manhood. It does take quite a man to remain attractive and to be loved by a woman who has heard him snore, seen him unshaven, tended him while he was sick, and washed his dirty underwear. Do that and keep her still feeling a warm glow and you will know some very beautiful music.

"If you truly love a girl, you shouldn't ever want her to feel, when she sees you greet a secretary or a girl you both know, that humiliation of wondering if she was someone who caused you to be late coming home, nor should you want any other woman to be able to meet your wife and know she was smiling behind her eyes as she looked at her, the woman you love, remembering this was the woman you rejected even momentarily for her favors.

"Mike, you know better than many what an unhappy home is and what it can do to others, now you have a chance to make it come out the way it should. There is no greater happiness for a man than approaching a door at the end of a day knowing someone on the other side of that door is waiting for the sound of his footsteps.

"Love, Dad

"P.S. You'll never get in trouble if you say 'I love you' at least once a day."

In 1988, Maureen Reagan organized a luncheon to honor Nancy and raise money for her campaign against drugs. As a surprise to Nancy, her husband Ronald Reagan gave a loving tribute to her when she came up to the podium:

"What do you say about someone who gives your life meaning? What do you say about someone who's always there with support and understanding, someone who makes sacrifices so that your life will be easier and more successful? Well, what you say is that you love that person and treasure her.

"I simply can't imagine the last eight years without Nancy. . . . You know, she once said that a president has all kinds of advisers and experts who look after his interest when it comes to foreign policy or the economy or whatever, but no one who looks after his needs as a human being. Well, Nancy has done that for me through recuperations and crises. Every president should be so lucky.

"I think it's all too common in marriage that, no matter how much partners love each other, they don't thank each other enough. And I suppose I don't thank Nancy enough for all that she does for me. So, Nancy, in front of all your friends here today, let me say, thank you for all you do. Thank you for your love. And thank you for just being you."

The Reagans' love is strong after many years of marriage. The two are dancing at a state dinner for the president of Algeria, 17 April 1985. (Courtesy of the Ronald Reagan Library)

[D]ay after day there were decisions that had to be made. . . . [T]he help I have found is in turning to God and asking His help in prayer. I believe very much in the power of prayer and feel if you sincerely ask for His help, it is forthcoming. . . . My faith is unshakable. . . . I thank you for a peace beyond description.

—RONALD REAGAN

CHAPTER 9

CALIFORNIA'S CHRISTIAN GOVERNOR

Be anxious for nothing, but in everything by prayer
and supplication, with thanksgiving, let your requests
be made known to God; and the peace of God, which
surpasses all understanding, will guard your hearts
and minds through Christ Jesus.

PHILIPPIANS 4:6–7

T he sixties and seventies would prove to be a very exciting time in
Reagan's life filled with many unexpected twists and surprising
turns. Reagan had committed his life to the Lord and trusted in Him even
when he didn't understand God's purpose, choosing to follow Him
regardless of where the path might lead—even as it led to the governorship of California. He heeded the Proverb that says, "Trust in the Lord
with all your heart, And lean not on your own understanding; In all your
ways acknowledge Him, And He shall direct your paths" (Proverbs 3: 5–6).

"Yes! Yes!" Reagan answered when the religion writer from the *Oakland Tribune* asked him if it were true that he committed his life into Christ's hands prior to the California election. He continued, "I've always believed there is a certain divine scheme of things. I'm not quite able to explain how my election happened or why I'm here, apart from believing it is part of God's plan for me."

"There's nothing automatic about God's will," he went on to say. "I think it is very plain that we are given a certain control of our destiny because we have a chance to choose. We are given a set of rules or guidelines in the Bible by which to live and it is up to us to decide whether we will abide by them or not." Once again, Reagan was echoing the words that his mother had long ago instilled in him—but now they had become his own.

FEAR OF FLYING

While Reagan worked for General Electric, he refused to fly. His contract explicitly stipulated that he would only travel by car or train. His fear, he thought, was perfectly justified because he had lost several good friends in airplane accidents in the early fifties. As Reagan says, those accidents "caused something inside me to say it wasn't a safe time for me to go flying. Call it a hunch if you will, but I felt that if I agreed to fly, I'd get in the wrong plane someday. . . . I knew that someday I'd fly again but I'd know when the time was right." So when Reagan began considering a run for California governor, he knew the right time had come.

Reagan became a Republican in 1962, after years of arguing the other side to his brother and other conservative friends, and by the mid-sixties he was frequently campaigning for Republican candidates. Just two years later, Reagan would make a speech and set the stage for one of the most remarkable ascensions in political history. Moon had introduced Reagan to one of his ad agency's clients, a man named Holmes

Tuttle who owned a prominent car dealership in Los Angeles (His brother Moon would again and again prove to be an important factor in Reagan's rise to the presidency). And in 1964, Tuttle asked Reagan to make a fund-raising speech for presidential candidate Barry Goldwater at the Ambassador Hotel. The speech was a huge success and well received. Mr. Henry Salvatori, a businessman and later Reagan Kitchen Cabinet member, paid to have the speech televised nationally, causing a wellspring of support for Goldwater from all over the nation.

In the speech, Reagan challenged Americans, "Alexander Hamilton warned us that a nation which can prefer disgrace to danger is prepared for a master and deserves one. . . . If we are to believe that nothing is worth the dying, when did this begin? Should Moses have told the children of Israel to live in slavery rather than dare the wilderness? Should Christ have refused the Cross? Should the patriots at Concord Bridge have refused to fire the shot heard round the world? Are we to believe that all the martyrs of history died in vain?"

"You and I have a rendezvous with destiny. We can preserve for our children this, the last best hope of man on earth, or we can sentence them to take the first step into a thousand years of darkness. If we fail, at least we can let our children, and our children's children, say of us we justified our brief moment here. We did all that could be done." Goldwater would eventually lose to Lyndon B. Johnson and fade from public consciousness, but no one would soon forget that speech and Reagan found himself at the center of the conservative movement.

And so, despite his fears, Reagan would have to fly again. As Michael Reagan tells it: "Dad was up in San Francisco, in Northern California, and Holmes Tuttle and some other men wanted to form a committee to support Dad for governor. But there was one problem; the meeting was scheduled in Los Angeles that next morning. Moon called Dad and told him if he had any thought of running for governor he had to take an airplane to LA to get there in time for the meeting." The rest, as they say, is history.

REAGAN TAKES OFFICE

On January 3, 1967, Ronald Reagan became the thirty-third governor of the state of California and took his oath of office on a four-hundred-year-old Bible brought to California by Father Junipero Serra, an immigrant from Spain. (Father Serra was the Catholic priest who founded the Missions up and down the coast of California during the eighteenth century.)

After giving a four-minute speech, Reagan turned to the minister who had participated in the ceremony and said, "I am deeply grateful for your presence because you remind us, and bring here, the presence of someone else, without whose presence I certainly wouldn't have the nerve to do what I am going to try to do." He continued, "Someone back in our history, I think it was Benjamin Franklin, said, 'If ever someone could take public office and bring to public office the teachings and the precepts of the Prince of Peace, he would revolutionize the world and men would be remembering him for a thousand years.' I don't think anyone could ever take office and be so presumptuous to believe he could do that or that he could follow those precepts completely. I can tell you this, I'll try very hard. I think it is needed in today's world."

Later that week, the new governor made these comments at a prayer breakfast: "Faith in God is absolutely essential if a person is to do his best. Sometimes we're afraid to let people know that we rely on God. Taking this stand just seems to be a logical and proper way to begin." He continued, "Belief in the dependence on God is essential to our state and nation. This will be an integral part of our state as long as I have anything to do with it."

Reagan's work as governor was predictably demanding and intense, more so than his duties as SAG president, but he still tried to maintain balance in his life. He exercised regularly and ate a sensible diet, and he preferred to spend time at home with his family rather than attending social functions. Nancy said of him: "Ronnie has never been one of the boys." Throughout his stint as governor, Reagan would usually go straight

The Reagans aboard a boat in California in the sixties. (Courtesy of the Ronald Reagan Library)

home after work instead of socializing with the legislators or press, bringing, as Nancy would reveal, "a big pile of documents to read at night."

Reagan worked wisely, was disciplined, and used his time well. "Instead of fretting over scheduling details," writes Reagan biographer Lou Cannon, "Reagan focused on communicating the ideas that had propelled him into politics." His secretary said he would arrive at work by 9:00 A.M. after reading several newspapers at home. Evidently he had learned from past mistakes in his previous marriage and spent as much time with his family as possible. He would often leave the office promptly at 5:00 P.M. and tell the men still working to "go home to your wives." They would ask, "But what about the work to be done?" Then Reagan would respond, "It's not that important. Go home."

The Reagan family attended worship services together at the Bel Air Presbyterian Church, where Reagan often sought guidance from

Reverend Donn Moomaw. Reverend Moomaw said in an interview that he and Reagan "have spent many hours together on their knees," and, in a History Channel program, revealed that Reagan would say in prayer, "God, I want to follow your will, not my will."

PUTTING FAITH INTO ACTION

Even while wrestling with the enormous difficulties of running a state, Reagan always found time to help the needy and would do extraordinary favors for people who asked. In fact, the examples of his good will are many. When a man wrote Reagan to ask for his suit to wear at his wedding (the man couldn't afford one, and he thought he and Reagan were the same size), Reagan sent it. When two sisters wrote to ask for a rocking chair for their mentally disabled brother, Reagan sent the man his own. When a young soldier in Vietnam asked Reagan in a letter to call his wife to pass on his love in case she didn't receive the card he had sent her, Reagan even surpassed the favor and hand-delivered a dozen red roses to the woman at her home.

In stark contrast to the majority of those in office, Reagan remained steadfastly devoted to what he personally believed the right course of action was, regardless of the whims of the populace. From the beginning of his governorship and presidency, Reagan made one thing perfectly clear to the members of his cabinet, as he writes in *An American Life*, "[O]ne of the first things I told the members of my cabinet was that when I had a decision to make, I wanted to hear all sides of the issue, but there was one thing I didn't want to hear: the '*political* ramifications' of my choices.

"The minute you begin saying, 'This is good or bad politically,' I said, 'you start compromising principle.' The only consideration I want to hear is whether it is good or bad for the people."

Reagan faced many challenges and trials throughout his governorship. In fact, when he took office in '67, he found the state budget was a disaster and had to resolve the crisis while contending with a Democratic-controlled state legislature. Also, the war in Vietnam was raging, and Vietnam vets were coming home to a less than welcoming country.

Reagan, unlike many in the country, had a great respect and admiration for those serving in the military and would hold dinners for returning POWs in California. Reagan describes the unrest at the California college campuses as "violent anarchy; the campuses were literally set afire by rioting mobs in the name of 'free speech.' Students had been beaten by literally lynch mobs for simply trying to attend class." There were bombings and attempted bombings. And police confiscated hundreds of rifles, pistols, and shotguns along with over one thousand sticks of dynamite and dozens of Molotov cocktails in less than a year at the Berkeley campus alone.

Reagan's own life was in danger when he visited these campuses; the rioters screamed obscenities at him as he walked by or gave a speech. Reagan was hung in effigy numerous times, and protestors even came to his home one night with Molotov cocktails, though their violent plans were thwarted by his security men. Ultimately, Reagan had to call out the National Guard to restore peace to the college campuses.

REAGAN REDISCOVERS THE POWER OF PRAYER

A few months after taking office, Reagan was diagnosed with an ulcer. He kept it a secret from everyone except his family but watched his diet and took a dose of Maalox every day. Still, the pain in his stomach worsened. What happened next he describes in *An American Life*: "A little over a year later, however, I reached for my bottle of Maalox one morning and something inside me said, 'You don't need this anymore.' So I put down the bottle and didn't take my medicine that morning. An hour or two later, I had an appointment with a man from Southern California who had a problem he wanted to discuss with the governor. As he was leaving my office, he turned around and said, 'Governor, you might like to know that I'm part of a group of people who meet every day and pray for you.'

"I was taken aback by what he said, but thanked him and said I also put a lot of stock in the power of prayer."

Later that same day, a man from Northern California came to talk to Reagan about another problem and, Reagan says, "as he was leaving, a similar thing happened: He turned around and told me that he met with a group of people who prayed daily for me."

Reagan later went to the doctor for his regular check-up and was told that he no longer had an ulcer. After running some more tests, the doctor told Reagan there was no evidence that he had ever had an ulcer. Of his amazing healing, Reagan says, "The power of prayer? I don't know, but I'd prayed daily for relief and I can't forget that impulse I had to stop taking my medicine, and then hearing about those prayers other people were saying for me."

Reagan believed strongly in intercessory prayer, and in one letter he thanked a couple for "telling me about the people of your church and your prayers for me," and noted, "I believe very much in His promise that 'where two or more gather in My name, there will I be.' I think I have known and felt the power and help of those prayers."

Years later, after Sister Mary Ignatius had written Reagan to congratulate him on his reelection, the president wrote back to her thanking her for her prayers, saying, "I believe in intercessory prayer and know I have benefited from it. I have, of course, added my own prayers to the point that sometimes I wonder if the Lord doesn't say, 'here he comes again.'"

Reagan's writings during this period of his life are full of expressions similar to this one: "I now have my mother's faith." After going through so many trials and difficulties in his personal and professional life, Reagan's faith had deepened. In writing to a member of the California Secret Service who had lost a leg to cancer, he wrote in part: "I'm sure you must have some low moments when you wonder about the why of things. I don't know that I have any particular answers to questions of the kind, and yet from the vantage point of thirty-one years farther on, I have discovered that I believe very deeply in something I was raised to believe in by my mother. I now seem to have her faith that there is a divine plan."

In another letter, he wrote to a young woman about how he had learned to deal with his struggles in office: "[W]hen I first got here and sat at the desk where I'm sitting now, I found when almost every hour someone stood across the desk from me and said we have a problem . . . the help I have found is in turning to God and asking His help in prayer. I believe very much in the power of prayer and feel if you sincerely ask for His help, it is forthcoming. For me that has been the answer." He also told her, "I have spent more time in prayer these past months than any previous period I can recall. The every day demands of this job could leave me with many doubts and fears if it were not for the wisdom and strength that come from these times of prayer."

Reagan was testifying that God's promise regarding prayer, as seen in Jesus' words in Luke 11, was true. He had seen it in his own life. "Ask and it will be given to you; . . . how much more will your heavenly Father give the Holy Spirit to those who ask Him!"

In a 1973 letter to the Cleavers, the parents of his high-school sweetheart and minister of his church in Dixon, Illinois, Reagan wrote, "One thing I do know—all the hours in the old church in Dixon (which I didn't appreciate at the time) and all of Nelle's faith, have come together in a kind of inheritance without which I'd be lost and helpless. During my first months in office, when day after day there were decisions that had to be made, I had an almost irresistible urge—really a physical urge—to look over my shoulder for someone I could pass the problem on to. Then without my quite knowing how it happened, I realized I was looking in the wrong direction. I started looking up instead and have been doing so for quite awhile now. My faith is unshakable, and because all of you were so much responsible, I thank you for a peace beyond description. Love, Dutch."

Reagan's letter to the Cleavers echoes what the Apostle Paul writes about in Philippians 4:6–7: "Be anxious for nothing, but in everything by prayer and supplication, with thanksgiving, let your requests be made known to God; and the peace of God, which surpasses all understanding, will guard your hearts and minds through Christ Jesus."

Dr. Charles Stanley emphasizes the power of this reassuring verse by saying: "'Don't worry. Pray!' Paul says. And notice the immediate result—peace. Even before our prayers are answered, there is peace. Before we have any idea how things will work out, there is peace. Why? Because by our crying out to God and unloading our cares and burdens on Him, He is assured of (and we are reminded of) our dependence on Him. And that is His priority; that is what pleases Him."

LOOKING TO THE FUTURE

Reagan was directly responsible for many outstanding, positive turns of events in California during his governorship: He balanced the budget, saved the state from bankruptcy, and laid the foundation for tremendous economic growth. But more important than that, he focused attention on the man who made his success possible, Jesus Christ.

During Reagan's years as governor, the "Jesus movement" was growing on the beaches of California. He liked what he knew of these people who seemed to be earnestly seeking Christ and, in writing to Billy Graham, said, "For a long time now I have been opposed to the young people's rejection of the church; at the same time they seem to be turning to Christ."

Reagan also turned his attention to the problems of drug addiction, which he discussed in a meeting he had with Pope Paul VI. Reagan said the Pope "had been most helpful to the United States in the international effort to reduce the drug traffic." Reagan continued, "However, he [the Pope] was concerned about whether this alone could solve the problem. I told him of my own feeling that it could not, that it was almost like carrying water in a sieve, and that only a program that would make our young people voluntarily reject drugs could eventually do the job. I told him of the so-called 'Jesus movement' in America and how so many young people had simply turned from drugs to a faith in Jesus. As you can imagine, he was not surprised, nor should we be, for He promised that He was our salvation."

Reagan realized early in his political career that the machinery of government could only take America so far and our most desperate need was a strong spiritual foundation. In 1972, at the Governor's Prayer Breakfast, Reagan spoke about his belief that God holds the answer to our social problems: "I think our nation and the world need a spiritual revival as it has never been needed before . . . a simple answer . . . a profound and complete solution to all the troubles we face."

And when he introduced Billy Graham to a rally in California, Reagan said to the crowd, "There is no need in our land today greater than the need to rediscover our spiritual heritage. Why is a representative of government here? To welcome with humble pride a man whose mission in life has been to remind us that in all our seeking, in all our confusion, the answer to each problem is to be found in the simple words of Jesus of Nazareth, who urged us to love one another."

Reagan had come far in his life, from being a poor kid in the Midwest to becoming a hugely successful actor and subsequently governor of California. And he knew it was all due to the gracious giver of all things. In 1973, Reagan wrote to his former Sunday school teacher still in awe over his tremendous success: "Every once in a while I pinch myself sitting opposite the head of state of one or other of the dozen nations we've visited, thinking this can't be 'Dutch' Reagan here. I should still be out on the dock at Lowell Park."

In a letter to the Cleaver family describing his years as governor, Reagan would write, "These have been eight wonderful years; challenging, exciting and yet with a sense of accomplishment that is most inwardly rewarding. My plans are going forward so that I can devote full time to writing, using radio and traveling about the country speaking on the philosophy I believe in and what must be done if we are to save this system of ours that has provided so much for so many. . . . I don't know what the future may hold for me, but as I say, I intend to hit the sawdust trail and speak out on the issues of the day for whatever that's worth or whatever help it might be."

Reagan's eight years as governor had indeed been challenging, exciting, and wonderful but were nothing compared to the road ahead.

I suppose it's the scriptural line, "I look to the hills from whence cometh my strength," I understand it a little better when I'm up here.

—RONALD REAGAN

CHAPTER 10

THE OPEN CATHEDRAL

*I will lift up my eyes to the hills—From whence
comes my help? My help comes from the Lord,
Who made heaven and earth.*

PSALM 121:1–2

In 1981, while President Reagan was recovering from the emergency surgery that saved his life from an assassin's bullet, he scribbled a brief note and handed it to one of his close associates. The note asked one simple question: When would he be able to get back to work on his California ranch? His beautiful Rancho del Cielo (Ranch in the Sky or Sky Ranch) was always on his mind. It was where he was able to restore his physical and spiritual strength.

Ronald Reagan renamed the ranch after purchasing it in 1974, the last year of his second term as governor of California. "From the first day we saw it," Reagan says, "Ranch del Cielo cast a spell over us. No place before or since has ever given Nancy and me the joy and serenity it does.

Rancho del Cielo can make you feel as if you are on a cloud looking down at the world."

The ranch is located high up in the Santa Ynez Mountains. On it, a small white stucco adobe house with a red tile roof looks out over a meadow and up to the oak tree covered mountains. From one side of the ranch you can see a vista of the sparkling Santa Barbara Channel. As you turn around, you can view the beautiful Santa Ynez valley.

Reagan was a true lover of nature. As Nancy writes in *I Love You, Ronnie,* his letters to her would reveal how deeply moved and interested he has always been in the outdoors and how he has always enjoyed gazing at its splendor. His daughter Patti says her father looked at nature with "an appreciative eye." And, as a child, she witnessed his love of nature when they would go horseback riding or he would teach her something new about the natural world. Reagan would often say, after showing Patti some new marvel of nature, "God thinks of everything."

In writing about God's creation while serving as governor of California, Reagan says, "Somehow I've never had any trouble reconciling spiritual and scientific versions of creation. God's miracles are to be found in nature itself, the wind and waves, the wood that becomes a tree—all of these are explained biologically, but behind them is the hand of God. And I believe this is true of creation."

Because of Reagan's passion for natural beauty, he always preferred to live on a hill and bought houses or ranches on top of them for most of his adult life. Nancy once told Patti that he liked hills because they were closer to the sky, and Reagan taught his daughter, "God is all around—everywhere, all the time. He just waits for us to turn to him. You don't need to reach up. You just need to talk to him, and listen to his answers."

Rancho del Cielo was a retreat for Reagan where he would go to think, talk to God, and fully experience His majestic creation. "He once called it his 'open cathedral,'" says Judge Bill Clark, a close friend and advisor of Reagan's. "He'd come out of the house and look at the sky and not say a word. The Great Communicator didn't talk a lot in those circumstances. Many don't understand that, but he would just look about him with that great grin." The ranch was where Reagan liked to go to "recharge his batteries," and his days and nights there allowed him to withdraw from worldly affairs and spend time in prayer and meditation, seeking God's will and listening for His voice.

Judge Clark says the two of them would often say the prayer, "Instrument of Your Peace," by St. Francis of Assisi while riding around the ranch on horseback:

> Lord, make me an instrument of your peace.
> Where there is hatred, let me sow love,
> Where there is injury, pardon,
> Where there is doubt, faith,
> Where there is despair, hope,
> Where there is darkness, light,
> Where there is sadness, joy.
>
> O Divine Master, grant that I may not so much
>   seek to be consoled as to console,
> Not so much to be understood as to understand,
> Not so much to be loved, as to love;
> For it is in giving that we receive,
> It is in pardoning that we are pardoned,
> It is in dying, that we awake to eternal life.

A Time for Work, a Time for Rest

President Reagan loved to work with his hands and enjoyed doing chores around his property such as building the fences at his ranch and found hard labor helped him relax. He did much of the renovation work on the ranch house soon after purchasing it, including the roofing, tiling, and laying the stone patio, and took a great deal of satisfaction from being able to see what he'd accomplished. The ranch house was heated by the fireplace, so Reagan had to chop a lot of wood to keep the house warm. In fact, a stack of the wood Reagan himself chopped still sits near the house. Reagan also made his own lake on the ranch, Lake Lucky, which he dug out with the help of his son Skipper (Ron Jr.) when he was a teenager.

President Reagan chopping wood for fireplace at Rancho del Cielo, "The Western White House," during his presidency. (Courtesy of the Ronald Reagan Library)

Reagan had found from personal experience that he needed to balance his life by eating right, exercising, and allowing time for relaxation and prayer. His ranch in the Santa Ynez Mountains afforded him the ability to do this regularly. Years earlier, he had worked himself to the point of exhaustion and nearly died from viral pneumonia. Reagan had learned it was important to pace his life, and often he needed to step back from the busy world to relax and contemplate. His ranch was his favorite place for doing just that. He found it especially easy to think creatively while riding his horse around the ranch and enjoying the beautiful scenery.

One day, while visiting the ranch, I decided to see President Reagan's favorite vista from his front patio. He had once said, "From the house we look across the meadow at a peak crowned with oak trees and beyond it, mountains that stretch toward the horizon." As I stood outside the house and looked toward his mountain vista, I was awestruck by the view. The way the trees line up on both sides of the mountain with the open space between them carries your eyes up to the horizon—up to the sky towards heaven. There at the ranch, the sky is such a wide expanse that it really does give you the feeling that it's easier to talk to God. You feel closer to heaven, surrounded by all His beautiful creation.

Patti says she used to watch her father when he stared off at the sky with a distant look in his eyes—one day, it finally dawned on her that he was praying and talking to God. In her book, *Angels Don't Die*, Patti writes that her father taught her prayer was simply talking to God, having a conversation with Him. Reagan proved to Patti, through advice and example, that prayer was very easy and uncomplicated, like talking to a friend.

One of President Reagan's favorite songs is "What a Friend We Have in Jesus," and its lyrics reveal much about his relationship with the Lord and the relationship Christ wishes to have with all people. It goes, "What a friend we have in Jesus, All our sins and griefs to bear, What a privilege to carry, Everything to God in prayer, O what peace we often forfeit, O what needless pain we bear, All because we do not carry, Everything to God in prayer."

THE WESTERN WHITE HOUSE

Reagan spent 345 days of his presidency at Rancho del Cielo, and it became it known as the "Western White House" during those years. Understanding its importance to his well-being, President Reagan always checked his schedule to make sure he would have time to spend at the ranch. Reagan was never more content than when he was horseback riding in a plaid shirt and a pair of jeans. He often said, "Nothing is so good for the inside of a man as the outside of a horse."

Though he came to the ranch to recharge his batteries, Reagan maintained an active work schedule there, hosting a number of U.S. officials and world leaders including, at different times, Queen Elizabeth and Mikhail Gorbachev. The ranch is not easy to get to. It's seven miles off a highway of narrow, rough road with numerous twists and turns on the mountainous ascent. Nevertheless, as the visitors who make their way to the Reagan ranch each year will attest, it is well worth the journey.

One of the comments I hear most often when people first see the ranch house is that they are struck by how small and humble it is—they expect the home to be grander and more opulent. When Mikhail Gorbachev visited the Reagans at the ranch, he said their home was "much too humble for a president." The original house was built in 1872 and, including an L-shaped wrap-around room built on by the Reagans, measures only 1,500 square feet. Of course, Reagan could have constructed an enormous, ostentatious mansion on the hill, but he felt more comfortable in this small, unassuming home and was proud of its modest charms. "This," Reagan would say, "is who I really am."

A MODEST HOME FOR A MODEST MAN

The home at the ranch was nearly lost to history in 1998. In need of money for the president's medical care, Nancy was forced to put the ranch on the market, and the Clinton administration refused to protect it like other presidential properties. The state of California was unable to build a consensus to save it. Fortunately, a small nonprofit organization called Young America's Foundation and its visionary president, Ron Robinson, stepped in to save the ranch. Today, my husband Floyd Brown serves as executive director of Young America's Foundation, and the ranch serves as the centerpiece of a program to train young leaders who share the conservative ideals of President Reagan.

When Young America's Foundation saved the ranch in 1998, Nancy carefully placed back their furniture and belongings in the house just as they had been while the Reagans lived there. Even their dishes are set on the table, and it looks as if they just stepped out of the house.

On the stone patio, which Ronald Reagan laid himself, sits the Mexican style table and chairs where, in 1981, he signed the tax bill that gave Americans their biggest tax reduction in history. President Reagan believed that Americans would prosper when the tax burden was decreased, and they did. The bill activated a ninety-two-month period of economic growth running from November 1982 to July 1990. This remained one of his proudest achievements.

When you first enter the small white adobe house, you find yourself in the Porch Room added on by President Reagan. The house still carries the colors (orange, yellow, red, and brown) dominant at the time it was decorated in the late seventies. The furnishings are in a western style with a fireplace on one wall and overcrowded bookshelves—filled with books on everything from early California and the American West to Irish traditions, animals, wildflowers, and horses—on the other. Native American artifacts and paintings of landscapes, horses, and cowboys decorate the walls, and a simple wooden table, on which the Reagans ate their meals, stands in the wrap-around section.

A step up through a doorway leads to the original part of the home, which is now a small kitchen filled with General Electric harvest gold appliances. Just as Reagan preferred this simple ranch home, he also liked simple food. In fact, macaroni and cheese was his favorite dish.

Signing the largest tax cut bill in American history, 13 August 1981. (Courtesy of the Ronald Reagan Library)

And on a table in the living room sits a jar of jelly beans, Reagan's favorite candy snack. Across from the kitchen on the wall is Reagan's "Jackalope," about which he often liked to spin a yarn. The creature is really a stuffed jackrabbit with deer antlers fastened to its head. Reagan had a great sense of humor, and you can see it all around his ranch.

In the master bedroom (one of only two bedrooms), the walls are painted bright yellow, Reagan's favorite color and a color that has been proven to have a happy, optimistic effect on people. The bed is covered with a beautiful quilt in yellow tones, and on a nearby table rests his and her Bibles, a gift from the Fellowship of Christian Athletes. On the wall is a watercolor painting of the Rock River in Dixon, Illinois, where Reagan spent seven summers as a lifeguard and saved seventy-seven lives. Also featured in the wall hangings are botanical prints of flowers with butterflies and cardinals, representing his love of nature. In the closet remain some of the Reagans' clothes; sitting on the floor are his riding boots.

Up in the tack barn are Reagan's saddles and equipment. The blue Jeep with the "Gipper" license plate sits in the garage along with his riding lawnmower, tagged with the presidential seal on the hood. Fragments of Reagan's life fill the ranch; objects that remain reveal his personality, his passions. Perhaps the most touching of these is a large rock found on the property which has inscribed on it Reagan and Nancy's initials encircled by a heart—all carved by Reagan himself. The rock, which now features the initials of the Reagan children and their spouses as well, is simply known as "heart rock."

President Reagan riding his horse "El Alamein," a gift from the president of Mexico, at Rancho del Cielo, 7 July 1983. (Courtesy of the Ronald Reagan Library)

All of us, as Protestants, Catholics, and Jews, have a special responsibility to remember our fellow believers who are being persecuted in other lands. We're all children of Abraham. We're children of the same God ...

—RONALD REAGAN, 1983

CHAPTER 11

THE ROAD TO
THE WHITE HOUSE

*Therefore do not be ashamed of the testimony of our Lord,
nor of me His prisoner, but share with me in the sufferings
for the gospel according to the power of God . . .*

2 TIMOTHY 1: 8

T he success of Reagan in national presidential politics tracked
with an unexpected realignment of the American electorate.
Arguments about what caused this realignment have filled volumes of
textbooks since 1980, but I wish to advocate a unique perspective that
secular university professors are unable to consider. Ronald Wilson
Reagan was the great communicator as we all know, but the key to his
political success was his unparalleled ability to speak the language of
faith and values. This ability was a result of his strong faith and close
relationship with God.

The coalition that had controlled American politics from the

1930s until 1980 is called the New Deal Coalition. The New Deal Coalition included blue collar whites in the north, white conservative Democrats from the rural south, farmers from the Midwest, and finally black voters in the large urban cities of the northeast. Republicans had been a minority party for all of those years. They mainly represented the interests of the elites: business owners, professionals, and the college educated.

In the sixties great social changes convulsed the nation. Our country was torn apart by the Vietnam War. This was the first war where, because of draft deferments for education, many of the elites on campus didn't support the effort. The sexual revolution was followed by the legalization of abortion and homosexual activity. These social convulsions changed the nation, and Reagan was able to speak to these issues with clarity and conviction.

Reagan was relying on God to give him the words he spoke. Like Saint Peter speaking before the Jewish Sanhedrin was "filled with the Holy Spirit . . . and able to speak with boldness," Reagan was relying on God to give him the right words to speak.

Because of his masterful use of language, he was able to unite together two groups which had previously been antagonistic and divided. These two groups were Catholic voters and Evangelical voters. Fused together, these two groups of Christians became the key to victory. Historically, when a leader had appealed to one of these groups, he had alienated the other. Reagan, however, used language, which brought these groups together and forged an historic electoral realignment.

The story of how he accomplished this feat began when he was running for governor of California. First, Reagan understood that the important swing constituency in California was Catholic voters. When he ran for governor of California, he faced a heavily Democratic state. The key to victory was finding a group of the Democrats who would vote for him. He found that constituency in Irish Americans. Two years earlier, this same group had helped elect another Republican Irish actor, George Murphy, to the United States Senate. The Reagan Kitchen

Cabinet and early staff were full of Catholics, and these same individuals helped play an important role in his run for president.

While Governor Reagan did run for president in 1968, it wasn't until 1976 that he launched a truly national effort to be elected president. In 1976, he faced a sitting U.S. president, Gerald R. Ford, for the Republican nomination, and his campaign strategy called for delivering a knockout blow to Gerald Ford in the early primaries of New Hampshire and Florida. The strategists of the 1976 campaign believed that those early wins would knock Ford out. But history unfolded much differently. In New Hampshire, Ford aggressively attacked President Reagan's calls for Federalism. Turning programs over to the states would lead to a dramatic increase in state taxes, the Ford camp charged. Tax adverse New Hampshire voters took the bait, and Ford won the important primary. Florida didn't unfold much differently. An aggressive Ford campaign charged that Social Security would be jeopardized if government-cutting Reagan was elected. Ford erased the Reagan lead and won Florida.

It wasn't until the Reagan strategists were desperate that they unleashed the candidate and won a smashing comeback victory in North Carolina. Turning to Senator Jesse Helms and his North Carolina conservative corps known as the Congressional Club, candidate Reagan even ended his speeches with a direct appeal to voters' faith. The campaign ditched the earlier ineffective TV ads and aired a thirty-minute speech direct from the candidate. This was so successful in North Carolina that the campaign aired the TV speech nationwide. The strategy worked, and Reagan won the North Carolina primary.

His new nationwide TV special invoked the biblical themes calling on Americans to keep their "rendezvous with destiny." In the final lines of this speech, he asked citizens to help him "make this land the shining, golden hope God intended it to be." After the speech aired, generous Americans poured an additional $1.5 million into the campaign. This resurrected a campaign that had been dead since the Florida primary.

Journalist Frank Van der Linden reports in *The Real Reagan* that Reagan met with George Otis of High Adventure Ministries during the campaign in 1976. When Otis asked Reagan, "Do you really believe somebody is listening up there?" Reagan replied, "Oh, my! If I didn't believe that, I'd be scared to death!"

In Texas, a must-win state for Reagan, the transformation of the campaign continued. Under the leadership of James Lyon, a Houston banker, the campaign opened the doors to a collection of conservative activists and Christians. The Texas primary showed the potency of this coalition of traditional Republicans and Christians. Reagan swept the state and took all one hundred delegates. Following Texas, the Reagan campaign used this coalition to win Georgia, Alabama, Nebraska, and Indiana. A winning strategy and theme had finally been established, but it was too late to win the nomination, which went to President Ford.

Nancy tells about the 1976 Republican convention in her book, *I Love You, Ronnie*. She says, "When we went into our box on the last night, the people just wouldn't let Ronnie sit down. They kept yelling, 'Speech! Speech!' Ronnie tried at one point to speak, but they drowned him out; there was no way he could be heard."

After the winner was announced, Ford invited the Reagans onstage, and, as Nancy recalls, "the response was amazing . . . so many people were standing there, tears streaming down their faces, absolutely silent, waiting for Ronnie to speak. You could have heard a pin drop." Nancy says, as they stood there, "Ronnie whispered to me: 'I don't know what to say.'" "And then," as if given words from above, "he gave the most wonderful speech," Nancy writes.

Michael Reagan also remembers that night after his father's defeat in 1976 and said something to me once that was very telling about Reagan's motivation for running, which had nothing to do with the status of the office or power for power's sake. Michael said, "After a meeting with Ford immediately after the convention, Dad returned to the suite where the family was gathered and grinned for the first time that day. He said, 'You know what upsets me most of all about not getting the nomination from the party and then becoming president? It's that I really looked forward to representing the American people at the SALT agreements with the Russian secretary general. I was looking forward to sitting down at a table and have him tell me through his interpreter everything the United States was going to have to give up to get along with the Russians. I was going to listen to him, and then, at the end, I was going to get up from my chair, walk around the table and whisper in his ear, "Nyet." I really am going to miss the fact that I can't say "nyet" to him.'" Michael paused and said, "Ten years later in Iceland he got his chance."

The morning after his defeat, Reagan met with a group of young volunteers, many of whom were weeping. "We've lost, but the cause—the cause goes on," he told the group. He then recited from one of his favorite poems, an old Scottish ballad he remembered from his youth. "I will lay me down and bleed a while/ Though I am wounded, I am not slain / I shall rise and fight again."

Van der Linden writes, "Although his followers wept in sorrow and frustration, their battered old hero accepted his defeat with the stoic calm and a serenity that arose from his faith in his destiny." Reagan said this about the loss: "If you've done your best, you've done everything you can for something you believe in, and if it doesn't turn out that is the course you follow, then I believe that means the Lord has a different purpose in mind for you."

To another group he said: "The cause goes on. It's just one battle in a long war, and it will go on as long as we live. . . . You just stay in there, and you stay there with the same beliefs and the same faith that make you do what you're doing here. . . . Don't give up your ideals. Don't compromise. Don't turn to expediency. . . . Don't get cynical, because look at yourselves and what you were willing to do, and recognize that there are millions and millions of Americans out there who want what you want, who want it to be that way, who want it to be a shining city on a hill."

Although President Ford won the Republican nomination, he was unable to beat Jimmy Carter in the November election, and it would take four more years of developing the Christian conservative movement before it would be able to win the election. After the 1976 campaign, Ronald Reagan became the acknowledged leader of the modern

American conservative movement. During the late seventies and into the eighties, the Christian conservative movement began to grow. Under the leadership of men such as Rev. Jerry Falwell, Dr. Tim LaHaye, Dr. Bill Bright, Ed McAteer, and Robert Billings, the Christian conservative movement (also known as the New Right) flourished, and between 1977 and 1980, Reagan crisscrossed the nation speaking to Christian and conservative organizations.

In January 1977, Reagan told one conservative group that conservatives were a potential majority of all Americans if they could only join together into a new and lasting alliance and shared his vision for the "New Republican Party": "It is going to have room for the men and woman in the factories, for the farmer, for the cop on the beat, and the millions of Americans who may never have thought of joining our party before. If we are to attract more working men and women, we must welcome them, not only as rank-and-file members but as leaders and as candidates. I refuse to believe that the Good Lord divided this world into Republicans, who defend basic values, and Democrats, who win elections.

He continued: "The United States must always stand for peace and liberty in the world and the rights of the individual. . . . [W]e recognize that we can reach our goals only while maintaining a superior national defense, second to none."

"When we are maligned as having little thought or compassion for people, let us denounce the slander for what it is," he told the group of young people. "Concern for the people is at the very heart of conservatism. Concern for the dignity of all men; that those in need shall be helped to become independent . . . concern that those who labor and produce will not be robbed of the fruit of their toil or their liberty. Concern that we shall not forfeit the dream that gave birth to this nation—the dream that we can be as a shining city upon a hill . . ."

Reagan often referred to America as "The Shining City on a Hill," a phrase that originally comes from Matthew 5:14, "You are the light of the world. A city that is set on a hill cannot be hidden."

In a speech given in 1969, Reagan said: "No government at any level and for any price can afford the police necessary to assure our safety and our freedom unless the overwhelming majority of us are guided by an inner personal code of morality.

"On the deck of the tiny *Arabella* off the coast of Massachusetts in 1630, John Winthrop gathered the little band of pilgrims together and spoke of the life they would have in that land they had never seen.

"'We shall be as a city upon a hill. The eyes of all the people are upon us, so that if we shall deal falsely with our God in this work we have undertaken and so cause Him to withdraw His present help from us, we shall be made a story and a byword through all the world.'"

He also saw America as a beacon of hope and refuge for those all over the world "who yearn to breathe freely."

At first, Reagan was not sure he wanted to run for president in 1980. He had passed the age when most men of his generation had retired. He was comfortable spending time at his beloved Santa Barbara ranch and giving speeches part time. The news media and a host of Republican candidates lined up against him were looking forward to using his age as an issue in the campaign. He knew he had been blessed by God with good health but still knew how grueling the demands of a nationwide campaign were. Seeking God for His will and an answer, he spent many hours in prayer before making the decision to run.

Ironically, when Ronald Reagan did decide to run in 1980, he turned to the same campaign team which had done him such a disservice in 1976. John Sears was back as the campaign's mastermind and manager. He again adopted a knockout strategy. Concentrating on the Northeast, Sears placed all of his hopes on winning early.

The knockout didn't come early as Sears had predicted, though. Reagan faced a defeat in Iowa at the hands of a much younger George Bush. Reeling from this setback, the campaigners fixed the situation more quickly in 1980 than in 1976. After the Iowa defeat, Reagan was unleashed on New Hampshire in a fashion similar to the barnstorming campaign four years earlier in North Carolina.

Then, a significant event happened.

"That winter," he recounts in *An American Life*, "a brief and seemingly small event, one lasting only a few seconds, occurred in a high school gymnasium in Nashua, New Hampshire, and I think it helped take me to the White House."

He was speaking about the debate in which he said, "I am paying for this microphone, Mr. Breen!" The crowds went wild when Reagan said this, showing that he was not one to be intimidated, and so did all the rest of America watching the debate on television.

Sears and the chief deputy Charlie Black were released from the campaign on the morning of the New Hampshire vote—a story that was almost lost in the triumph of the Reagan victory—and the march to the White House had begun with Christian conservatives as well as Catholics playing an instrumental part in nearly every state. In the past, Catholics and Evangelicals rarely supported the same candidates for political office, but with a growing moral consensus now concerned about such issues as abortion, the two groups were finding themselves bound together in support of a candidate believed to be of strong moral character. In fact, many conservative religious groups were formed

President Reagan addresses the annual Convention of the National Association of Evangelicals, Orlando, Florida, 8 March 1983. (Courtesy of the Ronald Reagan Library)

around the time of the election, including the Catholic-inspired Eagle Forum started by Phyllis Schlafly and the Moral Majority and Christian Coalition, both Protestant-based.

And Ronald Reagan was just the man to bridge the divide. Growing up in a family of both Catholics and Evangelicals, he understood the common purpose these two groups shared. He understood the orthodoxy of both, and he understood the language of both the American Protestant and Roman Catholic Churches.

This ability to connect with Catholics was on display no more clearly than in March of 1980 in the renowned Serb Memorial Hall on Milwaukee's south side. In a blue collar neighborhood full of ethnic voters of Roman Catholic and Eastern Orthodox backgrounds, Ronald Reagan was received with cheers and ovations. This was supposed to be a Democratic stronghold. Nobody could ever remember when a Republican had been received there as warmly as Ronald Reagan. "From the Serb Hall speech forward, journalists began to recognize his ability to connect with what would eventually be called Reagan Democrats," says Frank Donatelli, a campaign aide who worked the event and later served as director of political affairs in the Reagan White House.

What is almost universally misunderstood is that Reagan connected with these Reagan Democrats not because of economic issues, but because of moral issues. Polish, Irish, Lithuanian, Italian, and Cuban, these voters liked Reagan's stand against abortion and his ardent anti-communism. These voters didn't support Reagan because of his call for lower taxes. They saw him as a moral savior who had come to restore the moral consensus that had governed the country for more than two hundred years. They shared the same moral concerns with Evangelical Christians. The orthodoxy of the Catholic and the orthodoxy of the Protestant had come together when they faced a bigger dominant secular political culture, and Reagan was their collective champion.

By the Detroit Republican Convention, the race was over, and Reagan won the nomination on the first ballot. Candidate Reagan then made a move that surprised many by reuniting the party: he named

George Bush—his toughest opponent—as his running mate. For Christian conservatives, however, the real action was in the party platform. The Republican party dropped its longstanding support of the ERA or Equal Rights Amendment. The party also, for the first time, called for a constitutional amendment to ban abortion. With Ronald Reagan at the helm, the party was transformed, and conservatives grabbed control for the first time in the post-World War II era.

"It is impossible to capture in words the splendor of this vast continent which God has granted as our portion of His creation," Reagan said in his acceptance speech. He then continued, "There are no words to express the extraordinary strength and character of this breed of people we call Americans. . . . Some say the American spirit no longer exists. But I have seen it. . . . The spirit is still there, ready to blaze into life if you and I are willing to do what has to be done; the practical, down–to-earth things that will stimulate our economy, increase productivity, and put America back to work."

After finishing his prepared speech at the convention, Reagan

On the campaign trail towards the presidency. (Courtesy of the Ronald Reagan Library)

paused and said: "I have thought of something that is not a part of my speech, and I'm worried over whether I should do it. Can we doubt that only Divine Providence placed this land, this island of freedom, here as a refuge for all those people in the world who yearn to breathe freely." His voice cracked, and he continued on, "I'll confess that I've been a little afraid to suggest what I'm going to suggest—I'm more afraid not to—that we begin our crusade joined together in a moment of silent prayer." The once noisy convention hall became quiet. Then speaking softly, he ended with: "God bless America."

It was this sincerity, this openness, this commitment to his faith that gained Reagan the presidential seat. During his 1980 campaign, what the news media called Reagan's biggest mistake was really what sealed the Christian vote. The media blew out of proportion a remark that Reagan made about evolution. He became the butt of their jokes because he believed in the creation story of Genesis. What these liberal elites did not understand was that they were ridiculing candidate Reagan for a belief that was dearly held by millions of Americans. The more they mocked him, the more votes he picked up.

Nancy recounts that everyone knew Reagan would win the election after the debate with Jimmy Carter in which Reagan said, "There you go again," every time President Carter started talking about the nation's malaise. The nation liked Reagan's optimism and wanted a leader who had a vision of a brighter future for America. "He made people feel good about themselves and good about the country," Nancy says. "And quite simply, they liked him."

Jimmy Carter had won the presidency in 1976 by saying he was a "born-again" Christian, winning voters over with his sincerity to "clean up government." In 1980, the tide turned, and the important swing constituency of Christians helped put a new man in office. God used his people—both Evangelical and Catholic—to give the presidency to his humble follower Ronald Reagan.

If we trust him, keep his work, and live lives for his pleasure, he'll give us the power we need—power to fight the good fight, to finish the race, and to keep the faith.

—RONALD REAGAN, 1984

CHAPTER 12

FIGHTING THE
GOOD FIGHT

*I have fought the good fight, I have finished the race,
I have kept the faith.*

2 TIMOTHY 4:7

T he gray, overcast sky on January 20, 1981, was typical for a winter day in Washington, D.C. George Bush had just been sworn in
as vice president on the west side of the Capitol, while tens of thousands
of smiling people jam-packed together on the Capitol grounds and
throughout the Mall held flags and signs in support of the new president. They had been waiting patiently for many hours standing out in
the cold air, proud to be at this historic event. It was the day they had all
been waiting for.

President Reagan shares his own experience of what happened on
that day in his autobiography: "As I took my place, the sun burst through
the clouds in an explosion of warmth and light. I felt its heat on my face

as I took the oath of office with my hand on my mother's Bible opened to the seventh chapter, fourteenth verse of Second Chronicles: 'If my people, which are called by my name, shall humble themselves, and pray, and seek my face, and turn from their wicked ways; then will I hear from heaven, and will forgive their sin, and will heal their land.'

"Next to these words my mother—God rest her soul—had written: 'A most wonderful verse for the healing of the nations.'

John Barletta, a Secret Service agent close to President Reagan (who has traveled all over the world with him) has said that he too noticed this amazing phenomenon with the weather at Reagan's inauguration and other appearances: "The sky would be gray and cloudy at an outdoor event, and then when President Reagan came up to speak, the sky would clear and the sun would shine down on him."

President Reagan spoke mostly about the economy in his inaugural address, but also said, "I'm told that tens of thousands of prayer meetings are being held on this day, and for that I'm deeply grateful. We are a nation under God, and I believe God intended for us to be free. It

President Reagan placed his hand on Nelle's Bible while taking the oath of office at both of his inaugurations. (Courtesy of the Ronald Reagan Library)

would be fitting and good, I think, if on each Inaugural Day in future years it should be declared a day of prayer."

Later that day, walking through the White House with Nancy for the first time as president of the United States was a very emotional experience for Reagan. He writes, "For so long, I had shared the reverence most Americans have for that historic building; back when I was a kid in Dixon, I'd imagined what the private part of the White House must be like. But I had never imagined myself actually living there. Now, we had gone in the front door, gotten on an elevator, and we were here to stay— at least for four years." Then, as he notes in an *American Life*, "If I could do this, I thought, then truly any child in America had an opportunity to do it."

As Nancy Reagan points out in her book, "[T]he most striking difference between Ronnie and many other politicians is that he has never been interested in power for its own sake. . . . Before he was elected, Ronnie had always regarded the presidency with great respect, even awe. But when he became president, he had trouble believing that other people could be in awe of *him*. . . . Instead, he would refer to the presidency as 'the office I now hold,' or even 'this job.' For Ronnie, it would have been presumptuous to view his job in any other way. And yet he loved the ceremony of the office and the band playing 'Hail to the Chief.'"

KEEPING THE PEACE

President Reagan had the highest respect for the men and women serving our country in the military. In a letter he wrote near the beginning of his presidency, Reagan reported how he had started returning a military salute to soldiers by saying, "I want you to know it gives me as much pleasure as it does those young men I'm saluting."

Reagan understood, as too few do these days, the importance of a strong military for protecting our freedom and said, "We must make

President Reagan's last day of presidency, saluting as he boards the helicopter at the U.S. Capitol, 20 January 1989. (Courtesy of the Ronald Reagan Library)

sure the forces of freedom are stronger than the forces of slavery." So even as he hated to send our nation's young men to fight for our country, he knew it was necessary to keep the peace. "Freedom is a fragile thing and is never more than one generation away from extinction," Ronald Reagan said. "It is not ours by inheritance; it must be fought for and defended constantly by each generation, for it comes only once to a people. Those who have known freedom, and then lost it, have never known it again."

But Reagan was also fully aware of how serving the country was often difficult on families, and, in a letter written to a mother whose son was in the military, Reagan noted, "I shared your letter with Nancy. She cried, and I had quite a lump in my throat. We're parents, too, and we understand what you expressed so eloquently. . . . Your son has joined what I called the peacemakers. Keeping peace is the most important problem we face. And I believe that because young men like your son are willing to put on the uniform and endure the rigors of military life, peace is more secure."

War was always the last resort for Reagan, and, after the U.S. Marines invaded Grenada on October 25, 1983, he wrote again to the same lady: "I'm so proud right now of those young Americans in uniform I could burst. It seems that I've had a lump in my throat for the last several weeks. . . . I will be as careful of our country as I can. . . . Having to order those young men of the Rangers, the 82ⁿᵈ Airborne, and the Marines into a combat situation was the hardest thing I've had to do since I've been here."

In his autobiography, Reagan tells how after the military rescued the students and neutralized the Marxists in Grenada, he gave all the credit to the Lord, writing in his diary: "Success seems to shine on us and I thank the Lord for it. He has really held me in the hollow of His hand."

But no war, nor peace, was more important to Reagan than ending the greatest, most precarious war, of the last half of the twentieth century—the Cold War. Reagan sincerely hoped in his presidency to be able to open up Communist countries to economic and religious freedom. At a Young America's Foundation dinner in October 2002, Richard Allen, Reagan's first national security advisor, talked about Reagan's dedication to this fight by starting, "He witnessed the origins of the Cold War, the loss of all of Eastern Europe, the fall of Nationalist China, the Korean War, the Cuban missile crisis, and the beginnings of the war in Vietnam," and then Allen recounted a memorable visit he made to Ronald Reagan in January 1977. The men talked for hours, but, Allen claimed, the most significant thing Reagan said was: "My idea of American policy toward the Soviet Union is simple, and some would say simplistic. It is this: We win and they lose. What do you think of that?"

This was a startling proclamation, said the experienced political advisor. "One had never heard such words from the lips of a major political figure," Allen added, "and until then, we had thought only in terms of managing the relationship with the Soviet Union."

Allen continued, "Reagan went right to the heart of the matter. Utilizing American values, strength, and creativity, he believed we could outdistance the Soviets and cause them to withdraw from the Cold War, or perhaps even to collapse. Herein lay the great difference, back in early 1977, between Reagan and every other politician: He literally believed we could win and was prepared to carry this message to the nation as the intellectual foundation of a presidency."

In July 2003, I was fortunate to attend the commissioning of the USS Ronald Reagan, our nation's newest aircraft carrier. The ship's motto is "Peace through Strength," which was essentially President Reagan's guiding philosophy for winning the Cold War. In one of his last speeches as president, he stated, "If we have learned anything in the last eight years, it's that peace through strength works." And on January 13, 1993, in recognition of his success putting this philosophy into practice, Ronald Reagan was given the Presidential Medal of Freedom, the highest civilian honor our government gives to an American, for service to the nation.

AMERICA'S FALLEN

As commander-in-chief of the nation's armed forces, Reagan was informed of every death in the military, and Reagan would often personally call the relatives of diplomatic and military personnel killed in major accidents or in terrorist attacks, offering his heartfelt sympathy and kind words. When the KAL 007 airplane was shot down by the Soviets in September 1983, President Reagan was on his vacation at his ranch in Santa Barbara. Still, he called the families of the victims from the living room in his adobe home before heading back to the White House.

Journalist Trude Feldman wrote in the *World Tribune* about a special interview she had with President Reagan, one that had been scheduled in advance to discuss his approaching seventy-fifth birthday. Coincidentally, the interview fell on the day the space shuttle *Challenger* exploded, and even though Reagan was severely shaken by the tragedy and postponed his State of the Union speech, which had been scheduled for that evening, he didn't postpone the interview with Feldman, realizing that she was on deadline.

"When we sat down in the Oval Office," Feldman wrote, "Reagan had just finished paying tribute to the fallen astronauts, quoting the poet John Gillespie Magee Jr. and saying: We will never forget them, nor the last time we saw them this morning, as they prepared for their journey and waved goodbye and 'slipped the surly bonds of earth to touch the face of God.'"

Feldman tried to prompt Reagan to talk about his birthday. "'First I'd rather talk about the astronauts,' he said in a hushed voice, with tears in his eyes. 'Now they won't reach their seventy-fifth birthdays as I soon will. . . . I'm heartsick about the loss of their lives.'

"I draw strength from my belief in God and his teachings," Reagan told Feldman. "That belief and faith in the Almighty helps me to cope with a tragedy like this."

Reagan then admitted, "I wish I could ask my mother Nelle the meaning of this morning's disaster . . . With her goodness and her compassion, she would know just how to give comfort to the families of the astronauts and, well, even to all of us."

According to Feldman, Reagan finally steered the conversation around to his birthday to humbly say, "[T]he anniversaries of my birth aren't important. What is important is that I have tried to lead a meaningful life, and I think I have."

Joining Forces with the Vatican

In the summer of 1984, during the middle of President Reagan's campaign for reelection, the Pio Cardinal Laghi, the apostolic delegate to Washington, was traveling to Santa Barbara, California, to speak with the president (Reagan had gone to Rancho del Cielo during the time of the Democratic Convention to give Walter Mondale, his Democratic opponent, a moment in the spotlight).

Reagan had been the first president in American history to formally recognize the Holy See in Rome and had sent one of his closest friends, William Wilson, to be the first ambassador to the Vatican. Together, Wilson, Reagan, and other top leaders of his administration had forged a unique and clandestine alliance between Pope John Paul II and the American government.

This latest meeting in California between Laghi and Reagan was one of hundreds of direct meetings held between representatives of the American government and the Vatican during the eight years of the Reagan administration. And certainly the case can be made that the most significant foreign policy change made by President Reagan was his willingness to use the Catholic Church to forward American foreign policies, which also included listening closely to the recommendations of the Holy Father in regards to significant American policy decisions.

The substance of this particular meeting was very important. Since the crackdown on Poland's Solidarity Labor Movement and Lech Walesa and the imposition of martial law on December 13, 1981, by the government of Communist General Wojciech Jaruzelski, the American government had placed economic sanctions on the Polish Communist state. The pope was appealing for the relaxation of some of these harsh sanctions, which were having a negative impact on innocent Polish citizens, and President Reagan complied with the Holy Father's recommendation, as he had many times before. Back on that fateful night in '81, when martial law had first been imposed, communications between Poland and the Western world were immediately cut, and, in the weeks that followed, six thousand leaders in Solidarity were detained, hundreds were charged with treason, at least nine people were killed, and the Solidarity was outlawed.

President Reagan called Pope John Paul II, a native of Poland, and asked for his advice. At the time, most of President Reagan's top foreign policy leaders were Roman Catholic, including National Security Advisers William Clark and Richard Allen, CIA Director William Casey, Secretary of State Alexander Haig, and Ambassador at Large Vernon

President Reagan and Pope John Paul II had an alliance against communism during his presidency. Here, they are meeting at the Vatican, Rome, on 7 June 1982. (Courtesy of the Ronald Reagan Library)

Walters. Walters was sent to Rome shortly after America's crackdown on Poland and met with John Paul II and Vatican Secretary of State Cardinal Casaroli. They all agreed that the Solidarity Labor Movement, which strongly opposed the Communist rule, must be upheld and allowed to take root in Poland.

Six months later, on Monday, June 7, 1982, President Ronald Reagan and Pope John Paul II met together for the first time and talked for nearly an hour in the Vatican Library. Of course, the topic that dominated the discussion that day was the situation in Poland and the Soviet domination of Eastern Europe. Both men shared a fundamental Christian view that right would prevail over the atheistic communism central to the Soviet system. They also shared a view that Yalta and the subsequent division of Europe had been a complete failure and believed that if Poland could be freed from the Communist Bloc then other Eastern European nations would follow.

As National Security Advisor Clark has said on many occasions, "Both President Reagan and the Holy Father have survived assassination attempts, and both men believed that they had been saved by God for a special mission. They both believe that God had intervened to save them. This was a miraculous fact that both survived. As a result, they shared a unity of spiritual view and a unity of vision on the Soviet Empire. They believed that right would prevail over evil in the divine plan."

CIA Director Casey took the lead in developing a policy to help clear the way for keeping the Solidarity ideals alive in Poland. It was his strongest hour, and because of his earlier work with the OSS (Office of Strategic Services during World War II), he seemed particularly suited for the Polish offensive that was developed.

In the spring of 1982, President Reagan signed the secret national security decision directive (NSDD 32) that authorized a wide range of diplomatic, economic, and covert measures to neutralize efforts of the USSR to keep the people of Eastern Europe enslaved. This helped unleash the revolutionary plans for Poland.

The defense buildup of the United States, together with the development of the SDI, or Strategic Defense Initiative, made it increasingly difficult for the Soviets to match American military technology. The costs of defense were overwhelming the feeble socialist Soviet economy. The United States also moved to increase the economic isolation of the Soviets. The hope was that by depriving the Soviet leadership of hard currency and modern technology, their grip on client states would have to loosen.

Also, relationships with the Warsaw Pact nations were changed. These nations, in order to receive Western aid, were asked to protect human rights and begin a process of political reform. These measures were matched with increased funds to the broadcasts of Radio Liberty, Voice of America, and Radio Free Europe.

Finally, the president had special investments that he wanted to be made in Poland. He listened closely to John Paul II in making these investments. Using the Roman church and the AFL-CIO as his conduits of resources, he began covertly funding the now underground labor union Solidarity.

With communications cut, the best intelligence information coming from Poland flowed from a network of priests through Rome and on to Washington. It was at this time that Casey, Clark, and Archbishop Laghi would have regular breakfast meetings. Clark told me: "Casey and I dropped into Laghi's residence for early morning meetings during critical times. He would share with us his and the Holy Father's counsel. In addition, I would telephone him because he was in constant contact with the Pope."

Solidarity officials were hiding in many churches across Poland. The Holy Father encouraged the resistance on the part of Church leaders in Poland. Soon, the CIA was funding the purchase of printing presses, radios, and other supplies desperately needed by Solidarity. The CIA even paid the fines of Solidarity officials convicted by Communist- controlled courts in Poland.

In the years from 1981 until Solidarity was legalized in 1989, the United States worked closely with every level of the church in Poland to keep Solidarity alive. On February 19, 1987, President Reagan lifted the remaining sanctions against Poland after the government pledged to an open dialogue with the Church. Later that spring, Pope John Paul II returned to Poland. He was received by millions of cheering Poles. He had traveled to Poland praising Solidarity and calling for full human rights.

In December 1990, nine years after the Solidarity Union was outlawed by the last Communist regime in Poland, Lech Walesa was elected president of Poland in free and fair elections. The plans of the Pope and the president had worked.

Together, these two great men of faith had broken the power of communism in Europe, which led to the fall of the Berlin Wall. After their sharp, decisive actions, it was only a matter of time before Germany reunited and the Soviet Union collapsed. The story of their collaboration demonstrates a miraculous combination of creativity and intelligence as well as strength that could only come from the guiding power of the Lord. Both men understood the power of God and were willing to be servants to His will, allowing them to accomplish things beyond the pale of Man.

SPEAKING FROM THE HEART

Until Reagan became president, he wrote all of his own speeches. The demands of his new position required him to work with speechwriters to expedite the task, whether he liked it or not. Still, even in office, he wrote some of his major speeches, and he always contributed to his speeches by working closely with his writers.

President Reagan spoke from his heart and relied on the Holy Spirit to guide him to say and do the right thing. He had his convictions, knew exactly what he believed, and really believed what he said. That was one reason he could give such sincere and convincing speeches to his audience.

Peter Robinson, former speechwriter for President Reagan, gave an excellent example of Reagan's integrity when speaking to a group at a Young America's Foundation's event. Robinson told the story of how he had written the speech with the famous line, "Mr. Gorbachev, tear down this wall." President Reagan liked this forward demand, but others in the State Department and National Security Council thought it was too provocative and removed the line from the text. The State Department and NSC kept sending revisions of the speech with the controversial line omitted, but, as Robinson remembers it, "The president told Duberstein (deputy chief of staff) he was determined to deliver the controversial line. Reagan smiled. 'The boys at the State are going to kill me,' he said, 'but it's the right thing to do.'"

In his book, *The Bully Pulpit*, William Muir Jr., professor of political science at the University of California, Berkeley, speaks of the striking conclusions he reached in researching President Reagan's speeches: "In his eight years as president, nearly one speech in ten was devoted to what might be called religious discourse: orations at funerals, lectures to clerical audiences, and speeches on themes of professional interest to the clergy." Funerals and memorials, Muir continues, "offered constant opportunity to the president to speak of death's inevitability" and the brevity, preciousness, and meaning of life. "To put it into perspective, the quantity of Reagan's religious discourse," Muir continues, "let us compare his schedule with that of a previous president who was thought to be a devout man."

When comparing Reagan's third year of presidency with Carter's, Muir found an astounding difference. "Even though Carter was a self-described born-again Christian, he gave eleven religious discourses (and only if you stretch that term to the absolute limit), whereas Reagan gave twenty-four. More interesting, Carter scheduled himself to speak to no clergy." In fact, the only religious group Carter spoke to was a group of laymen (The National Conference of Catholic Charities), and even then he did not discuss religion and spoke at only one funeral honoring an individual. Muir reveals, "Even at the National Prayer Breakfast, Carter devoted virtually every word to questions of government policy."

His Quiet Faith Emerges

Belief and faith in God, and His son Jesus Christ, had given President Reagan's life meaning. This was the context in which he lived—trying to do God's will. Reagan's faith was a topic that was near and dear to his heart, and he was comfortable speaking about it to anyone who would listen. But, according to David Shepherd, author of *Ronald Reagan: In God I Trust*, it wasn't until January 1984 that the media focused on this fact—that Ronald Reagan had a specific and solid faith in Jesus Christ.

It was then, in the fourth year of his presidency, that President Reagan gave a speech at the National Religious Broadcasters Convention and spoke explicitly on themes which he had mentioned many times before, such as faith, prayer, the Bible, family, and the importance of religious values.

An editorial appeared a few days later in *The New York Times* saying, "Americans ask piety in presidents, not displays of religious preference." And a couple of weeks after the editorial, a reporter from the Knight-Ridder News Service interviewed the president and discussed his NRB speech. Here's an excerpt from the question and answer session that followed:

"Reporter: Mr. President, I'd like to ask you . . . a question about something that may be a little delicate, but it's nevertheless been on my mind and on the minds of several people.

"I was at your speech to the National Association of Religious Broadcasters, and as others have commented, you've never been much to wear religion on your sleeve one way or the other. But I wonder if . . . preaching the gospel of Christ . . . isn't a bit divisive and whether it might not be wise, especially since there are a heck of a lot of people in this country who are not of the same persuasion. It just doesn't seem like you in the past, and that's why I'm asking.

"The President: Maybe others haven't listened to me in the past. I remember once, long before I was even the Governor of California, when I was just out on the mashed-potato circuit, I was invited to speak to a national meeting of military chaplains. They'd been having a three-day meeting in California. And afterward, one of them came up to me . . . shook my hand, and said that I was the first person in their three-day meeting who had mentioned the name of Christ.

"No, it isn't easy for me to talk about this . . . but I do believe that there is, and has been . . . a great hunger for a kind of spiritual revival in this country, for people to believe again in things that they once believed in—basic truths and all. Obviously, speaking to religious broadcasters, I would speak more on that subject than I would, say, to the Chamber of Commerce. . . .

"The fall of any empire, any great civilization, has been preceded by it forsaking its gods. . . . I don't want us to be another great civilization that began its decline by forsaking its God. . . .

"I also feel that there is a responsibility in this position—as Teddy Roosevelt called, 'a bully pulpit'—to do those things. I was criticized for speaking about school prayer in the House Chamber at the State of the Union address. But am I not correct that above my head, engraved in the wall . . . was 'one nation under God?'

"Reporter: I'm speaking of a specific kind of religion. The allusions to the Christian gospel and to Christ as coming from a president who is a man in a nonsectarian office.

"The President: Yes. But . . . at the lighting of the Christmas tree . . . I said that on that birthday [of] the man from Galilee, . . . there are those in our land who recognized him as a prophet or a great teacher . . . and there are those of us who believe that he was of divine origin and the son of God and, whichever, we celebrated his birthday with respect for the man."

Attorney General Edwin Meese, a personal friend of the president's and who has also worked with President Reagan since the days he was governor, observed this about President Reagan's faith: "The president feels a person's religious beliefs are a very private matter. He had never tried to exploit them or utilize them for political purposes.

"At the same time, he feels a Christian has an obligation, when the opportunity comes up naturally, not to be reticent about professing his faith.

"Of all the people I've ever known, I have never known anyone less uncomfortable about discussing religious matters in a very matter-of-fact and confident way. To him, this is an important part of his life, and when the subject comes up, he is not at all hesitant to talk about it—and this was true way back in California."

President Reagan was a humble man and was careful to avoid making his faith an issue. David Shepherd pointed out that, during elections, Reagan did not campaign in churches. Instead, he chose to "address any Christian constituency from a public forum and discuss political and social issues that are of concern to them."

Still, the media attacked President Reagan for his talking about his faith and then, refusing to be assuaged either way, attacked him again for not going to church. In March of 1984, a reporter asked the president, "Are you going to church this Sunday, sir? The Democrats say you talk about religion but you don't go to church."

"Yes, I've noticed that," the president replied, ". . . I haven't bothered to check on their attendance, but I think they must be aware of why I have not been attending. . . . I represent too much of a threat to too many other people for me to be able to go to church. And frankly, I miss it very much."

Two Important Issues

On the National Day of Prayer in 1982, President Reagan told his audience: "I also believe this blessed land was set apart in a very special way, a country created by men and women who came here not in search of gold, but in search of God. They would be free people, living under the law with faith in their Maker and their future.

"Sometimes it seems we've strayed from that noble beginning, from our conviction that standards of right and wrong do exist and must be lived up to. God, the source of our knowledge, has been expelled from the classroom. He gives us his greatest blessing—life—and yet many would condone the taking of innocent life. We expect him to protect us in a crisis, but turn away from him too often in our day-to-day living. I wonder if he isn't waiting for us to wake up."

It's not difficult to detect from this speech two issues Reagan felt most strongly about, the first of which was school prayer. On May 17, 1982, Reagan submitted a Constitutional school prayer amendment to Congress to restore "the simple freedom of our citizens to offer prayer in our public schools and institutions." He was deeply disappointed when it fell short of the special two-thirds majority needed to win in the Senate but encouraged his supporters not to give up on the issue.

In a White House ceremony in observance of the National Day of Prayer May 6, 1982, President Reagan said: "Today, prayer is still a powerful force in America, and our faith in God is a mighty source of strength. Our Pledge of Allegiance states that we are 'one nation under God,' and our currency bears the motto, 'In God We Trust.'

"The morality and values such faith implies are deeply embedded in our national character. Our country embraces those principles by design, and we abandon them at our peril. Yet in recent years, well-meaning Americans in the name of freedom have taken freedom away. For the sake of religious tolerance, they've forbidden religious practice in our public classrooms. The law of this land has effectively removed prayer from our classrooms.

"How can we hope to retain our freedom through the generations if we fail to teach our young that our liberty springs from an abiding faith in our Creator?

"Thomas Jefferson once said, 'Almighty God created the mind free.' But current interpretation of our Constitution holds that the minds of our children cannot be free to pray to God in public schools. No one will ever convince me that a moment of voluntary prayer will harm a child or threaten a school or state. But I think it can strengthen our faith in a Creator who alone has the power to bless America. . . .

"Just as Benjamin Franklin believed it was beneficial for the Constitutional Convention to begin each day's work with a prayer, I believe that it would be beneficial for our children to have an opportunity to begin each school day in the same manner."

The other issue which stirred Reagan to passionate debate and activism was abortion. In fact, the only book Ronald Reagan wrote other than his two autobiographies was a small pro-life book entitled *Abortion and the Conscience of the Nation.*

Judge William Clark, a devout Catholic, discussed spiritual issues with Reagan as a close friend and writes in the book's foreword, "President Reagan's record of public service reveals throughout that no moral issue was of greater importance to him than the dignity and sanctity of all human life." Clark explains how Reagan came to his pro-life beliefs and states that Reagan was greatly influenced by his "devoted and devout mother Nelle" and his "fiercely humanitarian father" and, through his lifeguard job, where he saved more than seventy swimmers from drowning, learned "the value of each person's life as well as the power of one man's actions." These convictions, Clark continues, "were tragically reinforced by the loss of his daughter Christina, only three days into her life. . . ."

In January of 1984, again at the National Religious Broadcasters Convention, Reagan would state his views on the issue outright and stir up a lot of vicious criticism from the media. "Let's begin at the beginning. God is the center of our lives; the human family stands at the center of society; and our greatest hope for the future is in the faces of our children. . . . God's most blessed gift to his family is the gift of life. He sent us the Prince of Peace as a babe in a manger. I've said that we must be cautious in claiming God is on our side. I think the real question we must answer is, are we on his side?

"I know what I'm about to say now is controversial, but I have to say it. This nation cannot continue turning a blind eye and a deaf ear to the taking of some four thousand unborn children's lives every day. That's one every twenty-one seconds. One every twenty-one seconds.

"We cannot pretend that America is preserving her first and highest ideal, the belief that each life is sacred, when we've permitted the deaths of fifteen million children who will never laugh, never sing, never know the joy of human love, will never strive to heal the sick, feed the poor, or make peace among nations. Abortion has denied them the first and most basic of human rights. We are all infinitely poorer for their loss.

"There's another grim truth we should face up to: Medical science doctors confirm that when the lives of the unborn are snuffed out, they often feel pain, pain that is long and agonizing.

"This nation fought a terrible war so that black Americans would be guaranteed their God-given rights. Abraham Lincoln recognized that we could not survive as a free land when some could decide whether others should be free or slaves. Well, today another question begs to be asked: How can we survive as a free nation when some decide that others are not fit to live and should be done away with?

"I believe no challenge is more important to the character of America than restoring the right to life to all human beings. Without that right, no other rights have meaning. 'Suffer the little children to come to me, and forbid them not, for such is the kingdom of God.'

"I will continue to support every effort to restore that protection, including the Hyde-Jepsen-Respect Life Bill. I've asked for your all-out commitment, for the mighty power of your prayers, so that together we can convince our fellow countrymen that America should, can, and will preserve God's greatest gift.

"Let us encourage those among us who are trying to provide positive alternatives to abortion [crisis counseling centers] . . . I think we're making progress in upholding the sanctity of life of infants born with physical or mental handicaps. . . .

"Not too long ago I was privileged to meet in the Oval Office a charming little girl—filled with the joy of living. She was on crutches, but she swims, she rides horseback, and her smile steals your heart. She was born with the same defects as those Baby Does who have been denied the right to life. To see her, to see the love on the faces of her parents and their joy in her was the answer to this particular question. . . . Restoring the right to life and protecting people from violence and exploitation are important responsibilities. But as members of God's family we share another, and that is helping to build a foundation of faith and knowledge to prepare our children for the challenges of life. 'Train up a child in the way he should go,' Solomon wrote, 'and when he is old he will not depart from it.'"

Reagan firmly believed that if we couldn't reinstate the freedom to pray in school and couldn't convince the nation of the immorality of abortion, that we were in for a dire future. Again, speaking at the National Religious Broadcasters Convention in 1982, Reagan called for the need to have traditional values reflected in public policy and posed the question: "Do we really think . . . God will protect us in a time of crisis even as we turn away from him in our day-to-day life?"

He continued, "It's time to realize, I think, that we need God more than he needs us. But millions of Americans haven't forgotten. They know we've been on a toboggan slide, and they're determined to do something about it. And I'm honored to stand before you, thirty-five hundred of their most effective and courageous leaders. And let me say, I do not agree with those who accuse you of trying to impose your views on others. If we have come to the point in America where any attempt to see traditional values reflected in public policy would leave one open to irresponsible charges, then I say the entire structure of our free society is threatened. The first amendment was not written to protect the people from religious values; it was written to protect those values from government tyranny."

RUNNING FOR GOD

On March 2, 1984, I attended a dinner during a conference for Reagan's supporters in Washington, D.C. We were sitting and chatting around tables in a large ballroom when President Reagan garnered everyone's attention and spoke the following words, which can be seen to encapsulate the spirit and drive of his presidency:

"Fellow citizens, fellow conservatives, our time has come again. This is our moment. Let us unite, shoulder to shoulder, behind one mighty banner for freedom. And let us go forward from here not with some faint hope that our cause is not yet lost, let us go forward confident that the American people share our values, and that together we will be victorious.

"And in those moments when we grow tired, when our struggle seems hard, remember what Eric Liddell, Scotland's Olympic champion runner, said in *Chariots of Fire*. He said, 'So where does the power come from to see the race to its end? From within. God made me for a purpose, and I will run for his pleasure.'

"If we trust in him, keep his work, and live lives for his pleasure, he'll give us the power we need—power to fight the good fight, to finish the race, and to keep the faith."

Whatever happens now I owe my life to God and will try to serve him in every way I can.

—RONALD REAGAN, 1981

CHAPTER 13

A GOOD AND
FAITHFUL SERVANT

Well done, good and faithful servant; you were
faithful over a few things, I will make you ruler
over many things. Enter into the joy of your lord.

MATTHEW 25:21

P erhaps you have come into the kingdom for such a time as this."
These words were spoken to Queen Esther by her uncle Mordecai
in the Bible's book of Esther. Many of President Reagan's closest friends
and advisors have expressed similar words about his place in history.
"Clearly, Reagan was the right man at the right time, and history will
bear his name triumphantly," notes Mike Deaver. Retired Secret Service
agent John Barletta echoes this sentiment: "He became president at just
the right time, when America really needed him."

President Reagan certainly did come into office when America really
needed him. People often forget what the country was like at the time he

became president. There was a malaise in the country, the economy had hit a terrible slump, and unemployment was high. The U.S. military had been weakened, and America didn't appear to be the strong, vital country it once was. The Cold War was still going strong, and people were truly worried about the future.

Then, in 1981, Ronald Reagan became president and offered new hope and a plan to improve the situation in our country and the world. Reagan was earnestly seeking God's will for his life and for his dearly loved country. It worked. In a 1984 speech, he said, "Saint Paul wrote a verse that I've always cherished, 'Now abide faith, hope, love, these three: but the greatest of these is love.' May we have faith in our God and in all the good that we can do with His help. May we stand firm in the hope of making America all that she can be—a nation of opportunity and prosperity and a force for peace and good will among nations. And may we remain steadfast in our love for this green and gentle land and the freedom that she offers."

Reagan's vice president and successor, George H.W. Bush, called him, "A true American hero and a prophet in his time, a man whose life embodied freedom and who nurtured freedom."

Reagan felt called by God and re-committed his life to doing God's will after his life was spared in the assassination attempt. He fervently believed that God had saved him for a purpose. He came from humble beginnings but proved himself again and again to the richest and most powerful people in the world. Reagan's life from rags to the most amazing riches proves that God uses those who are humble and have the heart of a servant to carry out His will. "God does not always choose great people to accomplish what he wishes," says Dr. Henrietta Mears most aptly, "but he chooses a person who is wholly yielded to him."

Ronald Reagan then took his strong beliefs and convictions and communicated them to others in his unique and extraordinarily talented way. He used the gifts that God had given him in service of God's glory. The apostle Peter writes, "As each one has received a gift, minister it to one another, as good stewards of the manifold grace of God. If anyone speaks, let him speak as the oracles of God. If anyone ministers, let him do it as with the ability which God supplies, that in all things God may be glorified through Jesus Christ . . ." (1 Peter 4:10–11). Reagan also proved through his own faith and subservience that using the gifts God has given us can lead to unimaginable heights of success.

TEARING DOWN THE WALL

Without a doubt, one of Reagan's biggest victories as president was his success in helping dismantle Soviet communism. Years later, the effects of his presidency and life are still seen and still growing in the former Soviet Union. And although the gradual introduction of free market principles was a monumental shift in their culture and social opportunity, it wasn't the most significant change in the lives of the Russians. What was perhaps the most startling and inspiring transformation that occurred after the downfall of communism was the immediate religious renewal and growth that took place.

President Reagan believed that this kind of spiritual revival was what the people of the Soviet Union needed most of all if they were to turn their country around. Speechwriter Peter Robinson confirms this when he describes a meeting he attended with President Reagan. Someone in the meeting asked the president about reforming Eastern Europe and the role religion would play. "The president had responded with a beautiful little disquisition on the need for religious renewal in the Soviet Union itself, exposing an aspect of his thinking none of us had seen."

In the sixties, Reagan had often been a speaker at anti-communism rallies and, at one of these events, had listened as a man with tears in his eyes came up to the stage to speak. The man said, "I love my little girls more than anything. But I would rather see my little girls die now, still believing in God than have them grow up under communism and one day die no longer believing in God." The man's impassioned comment had a deep and lasting effect on Reagan, and he would share this story many times over the years. The father's concerns confirmed why Reagan would continue to fight so passionately against the oppressions of communism.

In a 1983 speech at the National Religious Broadcasters Convention, Reagan commented on the resurgence of Christianity in the Soviet Union and referred to Jesus as a hero who would be victorious in conquering communism. "Think of it," he boldly stated. "The most awesome military machine in history, but it is no match for that one, single man, [a] hero, [the] strong yet tender, Prince of Peace. His name alone, Jesus, can lift our hearts, soothe our sorrows, heal our wounds, and drive away out fears. . . ."

Since that time there has been a remarkable resurgence of the Christian faith in the former Soviet Union, and the Christian faith, which outlasted the seventy years of persecution and all attempts to stop it, is still growing. Philip Yancey illustrated in his book, *What's So Amazing About Grace?*, the difference less than ten years made in Russia: "In 1983 a group of Youth With A Mission daredevils unfolded a banner on Easter Sunday morning in Red Square: 'Christ is Risen!' it read in Russian. Some older Russians fell to their knees and wept. Soldiers soon surrounded the hymn-singing troublemakers, tore up their banner, and hustled them off to jail. Less than a decade after that act of civil disobedience, all over Red Square on Easter Sunday people were greeting each other in the traditional way, 'Christ is risen! . . . He is risen indeed!'" Being jailed for one's faith was a thing of the past.

In 1990, after his presidency, Reagan went back to the Berlin Wall—this time with a hammer and chisel. With a smile on his face, he hammered away part of the wall he had helped bring down during his two terms as president. Later, in 1994, when Reagan was eighty-three years old, he would write to Margaret Thatcher, telling the former prime minister of Great Britain that he felt "the Lord brought us together for a profound purpose." The two had become good friends working closely together for the common cause of defending freedom and bringing an end to the Cold War. At the time, a more profound purpose would be hard to imagine.

In March 2002, I was fortunate enough to witness Reagan's powerful legacy of freedom firsthand. My husband Floyd and I were on a cruise with Michael and Colleen Reagan, and the four of us were seated at the same table for dinner each evening. We had the same wait staff each night, and so, over the course of the cruise, we got to know them. The assistant waitress was a young woman named Tatiana who was in her early twenties and came from Romania, a former Soviet slave state. A few days into the cruise she found out that Michael was President Reagan's son, and the biggest smile spread across her face. She stepped back to look at Michael with a sense of awe, and for a moment, I thought she was going to bow down at his feet.

She said, "I love President Reagan! He freed me and my people!" She then told this to the head waiter, also from Romania, and he came over to our table and proudly said, "We love President Reagan in my country." We gave the head waiter a tee shirt that had a picture of the Reagan Ranch and a quote of President Reagan's on it. The next evening, he came over to our table with a big smile and said, "Everyone I work with is envious of my Reagan shirt." We were all touched. These were people who understood the value of freedom and the important role Reagan played in their own liberation.

GOD'S SOVEREIGN HAND

Reagan knew that the only way to be truly free was through the Lord, through the blood of Christ, and, paradoxically, through the sovereign hand of God. Throughout his life, Reagan could see God's invisible hand leading him, guiding him—God's tender grace was a place of refuge. The Bible makes many references to "God's hand" and the "hand of God," and in Isaiah 49:16, the Lord uses this imagery to tell the believer how important he is to Him, "See, I have inscribed you on the palms of My hands." Reagan was fond of this imagery, too—this hand of God, this hand of Providence—and it provided him an everlasting peace.

Nancy had trouble believing and trusting that God is loving and absolutely sovereign and He could be her source of peace. She was a habitual worrier. When Reagan was campaigning for governor and had to take up flying again (one fear that had haunted him for some time), Nancy was afraid that he would die in a plane crash. Reagan was able to set aside his own fears and comfort Nancy through his characteristically assuring letters, explaining to her, "God has a plan and it isn't for us to understand, only to know that He has his reasons and because he is all merciful and all loving we can depend on it that there is purpose in whatever He does and it is for our own good."

Reagan hoped to convince Nancy to believe and trust God "without any question or doubt" like he did. He dearly wanted Nancy to have the same sense of peace that he had enjoyed by completely putting his life in the Lord's hands. "He often wrote me of what was important to him in spiritual terms," Nancy notes in her autobiography, "and I admired his faith, although I did not share the firmness of his convictions."

Reagan was able to conquer his fear of flying and likewise his fear of dying because he believed in a sovereign God and completely surrendered himself to His will and service. Reagan was so dedicated, so confident in fact that after the nearly fatal assassination attempt, he wrote in his diary, "Whatever happens now I owe my life to God and will try to serve him in every way I can."

Many of his colleagues have remarked how amazingly calm and peaceful President Reagan was even in the most stressful situations. Says Mike Deaver, "Reagan had a profound spiritual faith that grounded him and left him with a nearly perpetual peace of mind. This is not to say he didn't have his moments of doubt and anger, but those times were rare."

Reagan knew God loved him and was merciful and therefore knew that he could trust in Him completely. In an interview in 1950, during his acting career, Reagan said, "I wouldn't attempt to describe what God is like, although I place my greatest faith in him. I think the wonderful line in the Bible which says God is love comes as close as words can."

Reagan became one of the pivotal figures in bringing peace between the two great world powers—America and the Soviet Union—and yet his peace came from an even greater power: the Prince of Peace. Jesus says in John 14: 27, "My peace I give you." In Colossians 3:15 we are told to "let the peace of God rule in your hearts." Isaiah 26:3 reads, "[God] will keep him in perfect peace, whose mind is stayed on You, because he trusts in You."

Probably the most well known verse about God's love for mankind is President Reagan's favorite Bible verse, John 3:16: "For God so loved the world that He gave His only begotten Son, that whoever believes in Him should not perish but have everlasting life." A friend of President Reagan, Herbert Ellingwood, said when Reagan was asked what that verse means to him personally, he responded, saying, "It means that having accepted Jesus Christ as my Savior, I have God's promise of eternal life in heaven, as well as the abundant life here on earth that he promises to each of us in John 10:10."

A HUMBLE MAN

Despite all of his staggering accomplishments, one of Ronald Reagan's truly endearing qualities was his humility—his remarkable ability to relate to anyone, regardless of class or social standing. He always tried to live by the Golden Rule and actually found it quite easy to talk with and relate to people of all walks of life, perhaps because his own life spanned both extremes. "He was indifferent to class differences," Ed Meese observes.

President Reagan was a very humble man even while he stood in the most powerful position in the world. "Nearly all men can stand adversity," Abraham Lincoln once stated, "but if you want to test a man's character, give him power." Reagan handled his power with the greatest humility. In fact, he had a sign on his desk in the Oval Office that read, "There is no limit to what a man can do or where he can go if he doesn't mind who gets the credit."

In James 4:10, the Bible tells believers to "Humble yourselves in the sight of the Lord, and he will lift you up." Humility is the sign of spiritually maturity. It's the realization that all achievement comes through God working in you and does not rely on your own power and strength. A truly humble person seeks God's will and asks Him for strength and wisdom, giving God credit for all the success one might attain. It's the challenge of not letting ego get in the way and remembering the biblical truth that "pride cometh before a fall." Because when we start thinking about our own greatness and not giving God his due, we stumble and fall. Reagan understood this from a very early age and was able to attain the greatest power by having the most humble heart.

THE GREATEST INHERITANCE

Reagan had grown up watching his mother taking an active role in the rearing of her boys while his father Jack took a more passive role. And so this

The Reagan family at Rancho del Cielo: (left to right) Michael Reagan, President Reagan, Cameron Reagan, Colleen Reagan, Mrs. Reagan, Ashley Marie Reagan, Ron Reagan, Doria Reagan, Paul Grilley, Patti Davis, 17 August 1985. (Ccourtesy of the Ronald Reagan Library)

was the approach he took with his own children. He left the majority of the daily parenting chores to the children's mothers, but he was an attentive father who worked hard to be involved in the lives of his children, offering advice whenever he could. But the most important thing Reagan passed onto his children, as his son Michael says, is a faith in Jesus Christ.

To this day, Michael Reagan carries on the spiritual heritage of his father, although it has not always come so easily. Michael has gone through some very difficult times but now frequently gives his dramatic Christian testimony sharing how God brought about a complete transformation in his life. President Reagan has been overjoyed to see his eldest son become a faithful follower—he and Michael and Michael's wife, Colleen, would often talk about their shared beliefs. Now, in the twilight of Reagan's life, whenever Michael goes to visit his father, he prays with him.

Maureen too had accepted the Lord and was able to die in peace when, in the summer of 2001, she succumbed to cancer. Her illness started as melanoma (skin cancer) but eventually spread throughout her body. Maureen brought a lot of attention to this terrible disease, encouraging others afflicted with it to catch it early and prevent its growth, and, when it was announced that her father had Alzheimer's disease, turned her focus and energy toward helping the Alzheimer's Association.

Patti had a strained relationship with Reagan and Nancy for a number of years, and it wasn't until later in their lives, when her father reached his eighties, that Patti starting mending the relationship, visiting them and speaking to him about the impact he had on her spiritual growth. Reagan was surprised to find out about her faith because he had always assumed she was an atheist. But Reagan had planted the seed of belief in her as a child, and it blossomed into a belief in God that endures to this day.

Reagan's son Ron, however, is a different story. In her memoirs, Nancy says the one thing that continued to worry her husband was that Ron Jr. would not go to church. Reagan enjoyed going to church every Sunday. In fact, at the time of Nancy's writing, he hadn't missed one

President Reagan giving a speech at the Berlin Wall, Brandenburg Gate, Federal Republic of Germany, 12 June 1987. (Courtesy of the Ronald Reagan Library)

service since leaving the White House and would go even when she couldn't due to illness.

In an interview on the History Channel, Ron Reagan talked about the rejection of his father's faith, which first became apparent one Sunday morning when the boy was just twelve years old. According to Ron, his father came into his room when it was time to go to church, and young Ron was sitting on his bed in his jeans and "not in my little suit." Ron told his father, "I'm not going. I don't believe it, and I'm not going." Ron admitted that it hurt his father very much, and he didn't think Reagan ever got over it. Ronald Reagan wished more than anything for his family to know the Lord the way he did.

END OF THE JOURNEY

On November 5, 1994, Ronald Reagan wrote a farewell letter to the public, announcing for the first time that he had Alzheimer's disease. In the handwritten letter he says, "I intend to live the remainder of the years God gives me on this earth doing the things I have always done. . . . In closing, let me thank you, the American people for giving me the great honor of allowing me to serve as your president. When the Lord calls me home, whenever that may be, I will leave with the greatest love for this country of ours and eternal optimism for its future. I now begin the journey that will lead me into the sunset of my life. I know that for America there will always be a bright dawn ahead. Thank you, my friends. May God bless you. Sincerely, Ronald Reagan."

Reagan wrote Lorraine Wagner, his longtime pen-pal, for the last time after this letter to the American public, in response to one she had sent him. In it, he thanked Lorraine for her kindness following the announcement of his illness and said, "With your prayers and God's grace, we know we will be able to face this latest challenge."

Ronald Reagan walked with the Lord throughout his life, and he could see the hand of God working in it to fulfill His plan and purpose. Reagan says he never felt lonely while in office, as other presidents have admitted. He knew the Lord was his constant companion and his heavenly Father was always right there with him to talk to whenever he needed Him. Reagan relied on God, developed a deep, intimate relationship with Him, and turned to Him for advice, counsel, and support.

In 1984, a man working in Reagan's administration died, and the president sent his family a letter of condolence. In that letter, Reagan talked of a poem about a ship, with sails billowing in the breeze, which journeyed out to sea. As the poet describes it, the ship grew smaller and smaller sailing away until it was completely out of sight. But just as it had disappeared to the one man, it was starting to become visible to others in a different place, "coming into view just as large and real as when he'd watched it sail away. It was not gone," Reagan said, "it had just gone to another place beyond our sight."

Reagan closed by saying, "It was the poet's explanation of death," and consoled the family by telling them their loved one "has gone to another place—the better place we've all been promised." Nothing better exemplifies Reagan's strong, unshakable faith in the promise of Christ's sacrifice. He saw death as a passage or a homecoming. He believed God would "call him home" at the time He planned for him.

Upon his arrival in heaven, I am sure Ronald Reagan will finally see his Lord Jesus Christ face-to-face and will hear Him say, "Well done, good and faithful servant. Enter into the joy of your Lord."

"We will dance with the heavenly host of angels"

MICHAEL E. REAGAN
June 11, 2004

Good evening. I'm Mike Reagan. You knew my father as governor, as president. But I knew him as dad. I want to tell you a little bit about my dad. A little bit about Cameron and Ashley's grandfather because not a whole lot is ever spoken about that side of Ronald Reagan.

Ronald Reagan adopted me into his family 1945. I was a chosen one. I was the lucky one. And all of his years, he never mentioned that I was adopted either behind my back or in front of me. I was his son, Michael Edward Reagan.

When his families grew to be two families, he didn't walk away from the one to go to the other. But he became a father to both. To Patti and then Ronnie, but always to Maureen, my sister, and myself.

We looked forward to those Saturday mornings when he would pick us up, sitting on the curve on Beverly Glen as his car would turn the corner from Sunset Boulevard, and we would get in and ride to his ranch and play games and he would always make sure it ended up a tie.

We would swim and we would ride horses, or we'd just watch him cut firewood. We would be in awe of our father. As years went by and I became older and found a woman I would marry, Colleen, he sent me a letter about marriage and how important it was to be faithful to the woman you love with a P.S.: You'll never get in trouble if you say I love you at least once a day, and I'm sure he told Nancy every day "I love you" as I tell Colleen.

He also sent letters to his grandchildren. He wasn't able to be the grandfather that many of you are able to be because of the job that he had. And so he would write letters. He sent one letter to Cameron, said, "Cameron, some guy got ten thousand dollars for my signature. Maybe this letter will help you pay for your college education." He signed it, "Grandpa. P.S. Your grandpa is the fortieth president of the United States, Ronald Reagan." He just signed his sign.

Those are the kinds of things my father did.

At the early onset of Alzheimer's disease, my father and I would tell each other we loved each other, and we would give each other a hug. As the years went by and he could no longer verbalize my name, he recognized me as the man who hugged him. So when I would walk into the house, he would be there in his chair opening up his arms for that hug hello and the hug goodbye. It was a blessing truly brought on by God.

We had wonderful blessings of that nature. Wonderful, wonderful blessings that my father gave to me each and every day of my life.

I was so proud to have the Reagan name and to be Ronald Reagan's son. What a great honor. He gave me a lot of gifts as a child. Gave me a horse. Gave me a car. Gave me a lot of things. But there's a gift he gave me that I think is wonderful for every father to give every son.

Last Saturday, when my father opened his eyes for the last time, and visualized Nancy and gave her such a wonderful, wonderful gift.

When he closed his eyes, that's when I realized the gift that he gave to me, the gift that he was going to be with his Lord and Savior, Jesus Christ. He had, back in 1988 on a flight from Washington DC to Point Mugu, told me about his love of God, his love of Christ as his Savior. I didn't know then what it all meant. But I certainly, certainly know now.

I can't think of a better gift for a father to give a son. And I hope to honor my father by giving my son Cameron and my daughter Ashley that very same gift he gave to me.

Knowing where he is this very moment, this very day, that he is in Heaven, and I can only promise my father this. Dad, when I go, I will go to Heaven, too. And you and I and my sister, Maureen, that went before us, we will dance with the heavenly host of angels before the presence of God. We will do it melanoma and Alzheimer's free. Thank you for letting me share my father, Ronald Wilson Reagan.

"There is a future for the man of peace"

GEORGE HERBERT WALKER BUSH
June 11, 2004

When Franklin Roosevelt died in 1945, the *New York Times* wrote, "Men will thank God a hundred years from now that Franklin D. Roosevelt was in the White House."

It will not take a hundred years to thank God for Ronald Reagan. But why? Why was he so admired? Why was he so beloved?

He was beloved, first, because of what he was. Politics can be cruel, uncivil. Our friend was strong and gentle.

Once he called America hopeful, big-hearted, idealistic, daring, decent, and fair. That was America and, yes, our friend.

And next, Ronald Reagan was beloved because of what he believed. He believed in America, so he made it his shining city on a hill. He believed in freedom, so he acted on behalf of its values and ideals. He believed in tomorrow, so The Great Communicator became The Great Liberator.

He talked of winning one for the Gipper, and as president, through his relationship with Mikhail Gorbachev, with us today, the Gipper and, yes, Mikhail Gorbachev won one for peace around the world.

If Ronald Reagan created a better world for many millions it was because of the world someone else created for him.

Nancy was there for him always. Her love for him provided much of his strength, and their love together transformed all of us as we've seen—renewed seeing again here in the last few days.

And one of the many memories we all have of both of them is the comfort they provided during our national tragedies.

Whether it was the families of the crew of the *Challenger* shuttle or the USS *Stark* or the Marines killed in Beirut, we will never forget those images of the president and first lady embracing them and embracing us during times of sorrow.

So, Nancy, I want to say this to you: Today, America embraces you. We open up our arms. We seek to comfort you, to tell you of our admiration for your courage and your selfless caring.

And to the Reagan kids—it's okay for me to say that at eighty—Michael, Ron, Patti, today all of our sympathy, all of our condolences to you all, and remember, too, your sister Maureen, home safe now with her father.

As his vice president for eight years, I learned more from Ronald Reagan than from anyone I encountered in all my years of public life. I learned kindness; we all did. I also learned courage; the nation did.

Who can forget the horrible day in March 1981? He looked at the doctors in the emergency room and said, "I hope you're all Republicans."

And then I learned decency; the whole world did. Days after being shot, weak from wounds, he spilled water from a sink, and entering the hospital room aides saw him on his hands and knees wiping water from the floor. He worried that his nurse would get in trouble.

The good book says humility goes before honor, and our friend had both, and who could not cherish such a man?

And perhaps as important as anything, I learned a lot about humor, a lot about laughter. And, oh, how President Reagan loved a good story.

When asked, "How did your visit go with Bishop Tutu?" he replied, "So-so."

It was typical. It was wonderful.

And in leaving the White House, the very last day, he left in the yard outside the Oval Office door a little sign for the squirrels. He loved to feed those squirrels. And he left this sign that said, "Beware of the dog." And to no avail, because our dog Millie came in and beat the heck out of the squirrels.

But anyway, he also left me a note, at the top of which said, "Don't let the turkeys get you down."

Well, he certainly never let them get him down. And he fought hard for his beliefs. But he led from conviction, but never made an adversary into an enemy. He was never mean-spirited.

Reverend Billy Graham, who I refer to as the nation's pastor, is now hospitalized and regrets that he can't be here today. And I asked him for a Bible passage that might be appropriate. And he suggested this from Psalm 37: "The Lord delights in the way of the man whose steps he has made firm. Though he stumble, he will not fall for the Lord upholds him with his hand."

And then this, too, from 37: "There is a future for the man of peace."

God bless you, Ronald Wilson Reagan, and the nation you loved and led so well.

"Neither disease nor death can conquer love"

PATTI DAVIS
June 11, 2004

Many years ago, my father decided to write down his reflections about death, specifically his own, and how he would want people to feel about it.

He chose to write down the first verse of an Alfred Lord Tennyson poem, "Crossing the Bar," and then he decided to add a couple lines of his own. I don't think Tennyson will mind. In fact, they've probably already discussed it by now.

Tennyson wrote, "Sunset and evening star, And one clear call for me! And may there be no moaning of the bar, When I put out to sea."

My father added, "We have God's promise that I have gone on to a better world, where there is no pain or sorrow. Bring comfort to those who may mourn my going."

My father never feared death, he never saw it as an ending. When I was a child, he took me out into a field at our ranch after one of the Malibu fires had swept through.

I was very small and the field looked huge and lifeless, but he bent down and showed me how tiny new green shoots were peeking up out of the ashes just weeks after the fire had come through. "You see," he said, "new life always comes out of death. It looks like nothing could ever grow in this field again, but things do."

He was the one who generously offered funeral services for my gold-fish on the morning of its demise. We went out into the garden and we dug a tiny grave with a teaspoon, and he took two twigs and lashed them together with twine and formed a cross as a marker for the grave. And then he gave a beautiful eulogy.

He told me that my fish was swimming in the clear blue waters in heaven and he would never tire and he would never get hungry and he would never be in any danger and he could swim as far and wide as he wanted and he never had to stop, because the river went on forever. He was free.

When we went back inside and I looked at my remaining goldfish in their aquarium with their pink plastic castle and their colored rocks, I suggested that perhaps we should kill the others so they could also go to that clear blue river and be free.

He then took more time out of his morning—I'm sure he actually did have other things to do that day—and patiently explained to me that in God's time, the other fish would go there, as well. In God's time, we would all be taken home.

And even though it sometimes seemed a mystery, we were just asked to trust that God's time was right and wise.

I don't know why Alzheimer's was allowed to steal so much of my father—sorry—before releasing him into the arms of death, but I know that at his last moment, when he opened his eyes, eyes that had not opened for many, many days and looked at my mother, he showed us that neither disease nor death can conquer love.

He may have in his lifetime come across a small book called *Peace of Mind*, by Joshua Loth Lieberman. If he did, I think he would have been struck by these lines: "Then for each one of us, the moment comes when the great nurse, death, takes man, the child, by the hand and quietly says, 'It's time to go home, night is coming. It is your bedtime, child of Earth.'"

"A life that achieved so much for all of God's children"

MARGARET THATCHER
June 11, 2004

We have lost a great president, a great American, and a great man. And I have lost a dear friend.

In his lifetime, Ronald Reagan was such a cheerful and invigorating presence that it was easy to forget what daunting historic tasks he set himself. He sought to mend America's wounded spirit, to restore the strength of the free world, and to free the slaves of communism. These were causes hard to accomplish and heavy with risk.

Yet they were pursued with almost a lightness of spirit. For Ronald Reagan also embodied another great cause—what Arnold Bennett once called "the great cause of cheering us all up." His politics had a freshness and optimism that won converts from every class and every nation—and ultimately from the very heart of the evil empire.

Yet his humor often had a purpose beyond humor. In the terrible hours after the attempt on his life, his easy jokes gave reassurance to an anxious world. They were evidence that in the aftermath of terror and in the midst of hysteria, one great heart at least remained sane and jocular. They were truly grace under pressure.

And perhaps they signified grace of a deeper kind. Ronnie himself certainly believed that he had been given back his life for a purpose. As he told a priest after his recovery, "Whatever time I've got left now belongs to the Big Fella Upstairs."

And surely it is hard to deny that Ronald Reagan's life was providential, when we look at what he achieved in the eight years that followed.

Others prophesied the decline of the West; he inspired America and its allies with renewed faith in their mission of freedom.

Others saw only limits to growth; he transformed a stagnant economy into an engine of opportunity.

Others hoped, at best, for an uneasy cohabitation with the Soviet Union; he won the Cold War—not only without firing a shot but also by inviting enemies out of their fortress and turning them into friends.

I cannot imagine how any diplomat, or any dramatist, could improve on his words to Mikhail Gorbachev at the Geneva summit: "Let me tell you why it is we distrust you." Those words are candid and tough, and they cannot have been easy to hear. But they are also a clear invitation to a new beginning and a new relationship that would be rooted in trust.

We live today in the world that Ronald Reagan began to reshape with those words. It is a very different world with different challenges and new dangers. All in all, however, it is one of greater freedom and prosperity, one more hopeful than the world he inherited on becoming president.

As prime minister, I worked closely with Ronald Reagan for eight of the most important years of all our lives. We talked regularly both before and after his presidency. And I have had time and cause to reflect on what made him a great president.

Ronald Reagan knew his own mind. He had firm principles—and, I believe, right ones. He expounded them clearly; he acted upon them decisively.

When the world threw problems at the White House, he was not baffled, or disorientated, or overwhelmed. He knew almost instinctively what to do.

When his aides were preparing option papers for his decision, they were able to cut out entire rafts of proposals that they knew "the Old Man" would never wear.

When his allies came under Soviet or domestic pressure, they could look confidently to Washington for firm leadership.

And when his enemies tested American resolve, they soon discovered that his resolve was firm and unyielding.

Yet his ideas, though clear, were never simplistic. He saw the many sides of truth.

Yes, he warned that the Soviet Union had an insatiable drive for military power and territorial expansion, but he also sensed it was being eaten away by systemic failures impossible to reform.

Yes, he did not shrink from denouncing Moscow's "evil empire." But he realized that a man of goodwill might nonetheless emerge from within its dark corridors.

So the president resisted Soviet expansion and pressed down on Soviet weakness at every point until the day came when communism began to collapse beneath the combined weight of these pressures and its own failures. And when a man of goodwill did emerge from the ruins, President Reagan stepped forward to shake his hand and to offer sincere cooperation.

Nothing was more typical of Ronald Reagan than that large-hearted magnanimity—and nothing was more American.

Therein lies perhaps the final explanation of his achievements. Ronald Reagan carried the American people with him in his great endeavors because there was perfect sympathy between them. He and they loved America and what it stands for—freedom and opportunity for ordinary people.

As an actor in Hollywood's golden age, he helped to make the American dream live for millions all over the globe. His own life was a fulfillment of that dream. He never succumbed to the embarrassment some people feel about an honest expression of love of country.

He was able to say "God Bless America" with equal fervor in public and in private. And so he was able to call confidently upon his fellow countrymen to make sacrifices for America—and to make sacrifices for those who looked to America for hope and rescue.

With the lever of American patriotism, he lifted up the world. And so today, the world—in Prague, in Budapest, in Warsaw, in Sofia, in

Bucharest, in Kiev, and in Moscow itself—the world mourns the passing of the Great Liberator and echoes his prayer "God Bless America."

Ronald Reagan's life was rich not only in public achievement but also in private happiness. Indeed, his public achievements were rooted in his private happiness. The great turning point of his life was his meeting and marriage with Nancy.

On that we have the plain testimony of a loving and grateful husband: "Nancy came along and saved my soul." We share her grief today. But we also share her pride—and the grief and pride of Ronnie's children.

For the final years of his life, Ronnie's mind was clouded by illness. That cloud has now lifted. He is himself again—more himself than at any time on this earth. For we may be sure that the Big Fella Upstairs never forgets those who remember Him. And as the last journey of this faithful pilgrim took him beyond the sunset, and as heaven's morning broke, I like to think—in the words of Bunyan—that "all the trumpets sounded on the other side."

We here still move in twilight. But we have one beacon to guide us that Ronald Reagan never had. We have his example. Let us give thanks today for a life that achieved so much for all of God's children.

"Angered by injustice and frightened by nothing"

GEORGE W. BUSH
June 11, 2004

Mrs. Reagan, Patti, Michael, and Ron, members of the Reagan family, distinguished guests, including our presidents and first ladies, the Rev. [John] Danforth, fellow citizens, we lost Ronald Reagan only days ago, but we have missed him for a long time. We have missed his kindly presence, that reassuring voice and the happy ending we had wished for him.

It has been ten years since he said his own farewell, yet it is still very sad and hard to let him go.

Ronald Reagan belongs to the ages now, but we preferred it when he belonged to us.

In a life of good fortune, he valued above all the gracious gift of his wife, Nancy. During his career, Ronald Reagan passed through a thousand crowded places, but there was only one person, he said, who could make him lonely by just leaving the room.

America honors you, Nancy, for the loyalty and love you gave this man on a wonderful journey and to that journey's end.

Today, our whole nation grieves with you and your family.

When the sun sets tonight off the coast of California and we lay to rest our fortieth president, a great American story will close.

The second son of Nelle and Jack Reagan first knew the world as a place of open plains, quiet streets, gaslit rooms, and carriages drawn by horse.

If you could go back to the Dixon, Illinois, of 1922, you'd find a boy of eleven, reading adventure stories at the public library or running with his brother, Neil, along Rock River and coming home to a little house on Hennepin Avenue.

That town was the kind of place he remembered where you prayed side by side with your neighbors. And if things were going wrong for them, you prayed for them and knew they'd pray for you if things went wrong for you.

The Reagan family would see its share of hardship, struggle, and uncertainty.

And out of that circumstance came a young man of steadiness, calm, and a cheerful confidence that life would bring good things.

The qualities all of us have seen in Ronald Reagan were first spotted seventy and eighty years ago. As the lifeguard in Lowell Park, he was the protector, keeping an eye out for trouble.

As a sports announcer on the radio, he was the friendly voice that made you see the game as he did.

As an actor, he was the handsome, all-American good guy, which in his case required knowing his lines and being himself.

Along the way certain convictions were formed and fixed in the man.

Ronald Reagan believed that everything happens for a reason and that we should strive to know and do the will of God. He believed that the gentleman always does the kindest thing. He believed that people were basically good and had the right to be free. He believed that bigotry and prejudice were the worst things a person could be guilty of. He believed in the golden rule and in the power of prayer. He believed that America was not just a place in the world, but the hope of the world.

And he believed in taking a break now and then, because, as he said, there's nothing better for the inside of a man than the outside of a horse.

Ronald Reagan spent decades in the film industry and in politics, fields known on occasion to change a man. But not this man. From

Dixon to Des Moines to Hollywood to Sacramento to Washington DC, all who met him remembered the same sincere, honest, upright fellow.

Ronald Reagan's deepest beliefs never had much to do with fashion or convenience. His convictions were always politely stated, affably argued, and as firm and straight as the columns of this cathedral.

There came a point in Ronald Reagan's film career when people started seeing a future beyond the movies. The actor Robert Cummings recalled one occasion: "I was sitting around the set with all these people, and we were listening to Ronnie, quite absorbed. I said, 'Ron, have you ever considered some day becoming president?'

"He said, 'President of what?'

"'President of the United States,' I said.

"And he said, 'What's the matter? Don't you like my acting either?'"

The clarity and intensity of Ronald Reagan's convictions led to speaking engagements around the country, and a new following he did not seek or expect.

He often began his speeches by saying, "I'm going to talk about controversial things." And then he spoke of communist rulers as slave masters, of a government in Washington that had far overstepped its proper limits, of a time for choosing that was drawing near.

In the space of a few years, he took ideas and principles that were mainly found in journals and books and turned them into a broad, hopeful movement ready to govern.

As soon as Ronald Reagan became California's governor, observers saw a star in the west, tanned, well-tailored, in command, and on his way. In the 1960s, his friend Bill Buckley wrote, "Reagan is indisputably a part of America, and he may become a part of American history."

Ronald Reagan's moment arrived in 1980. He came out ahead of some very good men, including one from Plains [Georgia] and one from Houston. What followed was one of the decisive decades of the century as the convictions that shaped the president began to shape the times.

He came to office with great hopes for America. And more than hopes. Like the president he had revered and once saw in person, Franklin Roosevelt, Ronald Reagan matched an optimistic temperament with bold, persistent action.

President Reagan was optimistic about the great promise of economic reform, and he acted to restore the rewards and spirit of enterprise. He was optimistic that a strong America could advance the peace, and he acted to build the strength that mission required.

He was optimistic that liberty would thrive wherever it was planted, and he acted to defend liberty wherever it was threatened.

And Ronald Reagan believed in the power of truth in the conduct of world affairs. When he saw evil camped across the horizon, he called that evil by its name.

There were no doubters in the prisons and gulags, where dissidents spread the news, tapping to each other in code what the American president had dared to say. There were no doubters in the shipyards and churches and secret labor meetings where brave men and women began to hear the creaking and rumbling of a collapsing empire. And there were no doubters among those who swung hammers at the hated wall that the first and hardest blow had been struck by President Ronald Reagan.

The ideology he opposed throughout his political life insisted that history was moved by impersonal tides and unalterable fates. Ronald Reagan believed instead in the courage and triumph of free men, and we believe it all the more because we saw that courage in him.

As he showed what a president should be, he also showed us what a man should be.

Ronald Reagan carried himself, even in the most powerful office, with the decency and attention to small kindnesses that also define a good life.

He was a courtly, gentle, and considerate man, never known to slight or embarrass others.

Many people across the country cherish letters he wrote in his own hand to family members on important occasions, to old friends dealing with sickness and loss, to strangers with questions about his days in Hollywood.

A boy once wrote to him requesting federal assistance to help clean up his bedroom.

The president replied that, "Unfortunately, funds are dangerously low."

He continued, "I'm sure your mother was fully justified in proclaiming your room a disaster; therefore, you are in an excellent position to launch another volunteer program in our nation. Congratulations."

See, our fortieth president wore his title lightly, and it fit like a white Stetson.

In the end, through his belief in our country and his love for our country, he became an enduring symbol of our country.

We think of the steady stride, that tilt of the head and snap of the salute, the big screen smile and the glint in his Irish eyes when a story came to mind.

We think of a man advancing in years with the sweetness and sincerity of a scout saying the pledge. We think of that grave expression that sometimes came over his face, the seriousness of a man angered by injustice and frightened by nothing.

We know, as he always said, that America's best days are ahead of us. But with Ronald Reagan's passing, some very fine days are behind us. And that is worth our tears.

Americans saw death approach Ronald Reagan twice in a moment of violence and then in the years of departing light. He met both with courage and grace. In these trials, he showed how a man so enchanted by life can be at peace with life's end.

And where does that strength come from? Where is that courage learned? It is the faith of a boy who read the Bible with his mom. It is the faith of a man lying in an operating room who prayed for the one who shot him before he prayed for himself. It is the faith of a man with a fearful illness who waited on the Lord to call him home.

Now death has done all that death can do, and as Ronald Wilson Reagan goes his way, we are left with the joyful hope he shared.

In his last years, he saw through a glass darkly. Now he sees his savior face to face.

And we look for that fine day when we will see him again, all weariness gone, clear of mind, strong and sure and smiling again, and the sorrow of this parting gone forever.

May God bless Ronald Reagan and the country he loved.

ACKNOWLEDGMENTS

This book would not have been possible without the help of many friends, family, and important Reagan admirers. First let me thank Joseph Farah and the staff of Thomas Nelson, especially David Dunham, Joel Miller, and Wes Driver. They were all of tremendous help with editorial comments, encouragement, and keen insights. This is the first time I have written a full-length book, and Frank York was my constant help. Frank York offered many suggestions to polish the manuscript and tighten the story.

Next, I would like to recognize Michael and Colleen Reagan. These two champions of the Reagan legacy provided my inspiration. I decided to write this book while cruising in Alaska with the Reagans, and I know I would not have had the courage to do it without their enthusiasm.

I also want to thank the staff of the Young America's Foundation. Without the leadership of Ron Robinson in saving the Reagan Ranch for future generations, most of my research would have been impossible. Many of my key interviews were conducted as individuals came to visit the Reagan Ranch here in Santa Barbara. Everyone in the organization, but especially Marilyn Fisher and Andrew Coffin, helped me gather information and photographs. Also I would like to remember the recently departed patriot Alice Atkinson who funded acquiring the Lorraine Wagner collection for Young America's Foundation.

John Barletta was nearly always with President Reagan during the years he was in office. As a Secret Service agent he knows more about President Reagan than anyone else I know outside the family. Since I moved to Santa Barbara, John has become a close and dear friend. John, you are special.

Steve Malone of the *Santa Barbara News-Press* photographed the president every time he came to Santa Barbara. Steve, I thank you for your insight and help.

Every person benefits from encouragement. Other individuals that have encouraged me are Michelle Easton of the Clare Boothe Luce Institute, Stephen Clouse of Stephen Clouse and Associates, and David Bossie of Citizens United. All have encouraged me to reach my potential as a writer.

Also, when this project seemed too big to finish, I would find encouragement from many others including friends from my church, Calvary Chapel Santa Barbara, and at my daughter's school, Coastline Christian Academy.

I want to thank Mrs. Reagan and Patti Davis for providing valuable insights in their previous writings. And the Ronald Reagan Presidential Foundation and Library in Simi Valley, California, has provided immense help to the project.

Finally, Dr. Tim and Beverly LaHaye suggested to me and my husband that this book be written. I admire the LaHayes. They have had such a big impact on my family through their writings, example, and leadership.

— *Mary Beth Brown*
SANTA BARBARA, CALIFORNIA

BIBLIOGRAPHY

Adler, Bill. *The Uncommon Wisdom of Ronald Reagan.* Boston, Massachusetts: Little, Brown, and Company, 1996.

Angelo, Bonnie. *First Mothers.* New York: HarperCollins Publishers Inc., 2000.

Bernstein, Carl. "The Secret Holy Alliance." *Time.* 24 February1992,Vol. 139, No. 8.

Busch, Andrew E. *Ronald Reagan and the Politics of Freedom.* Oxford, England: Rowman and Littlefield Publishers, Inc., 2001.

Cannon, Lou. *Governor Reagan: His Rise to Power.* New York: Public Affairs, 2003.

Colson, Charles. *Kingdoms in Conflict.* New York: William Morrow and Zondervan Publishing House, 1987.

Davis, Patti. *Angels Don't Die.* New York: HarperCollins Publishing, Inc., 1995.

Deaver, Michael K. *A Different Drummer: My Thirty Years with Ronald Reagan.* New York: HarperCollins Publishers Inc., 2001.

"Disciples of Christ." *Encyclopedia Britannica.* 1979 ed.

Dobson, James. *When God Doesn't Make Sense.* Wheaton, Illinois: Tyndale House Publishers Inc., 1993.

D'Souza, Dinesh. *How an Ordinary Man Became an Extraordinary Leader.* New York: The Free Press, 1997.

Dunn, Charles. "Faith, Freedom, and the Future." *Vision and Values.* Grove City College: October 2003, Vol. 11, No. 2.

Edwards, Anne. *Early Reagan.* New York: William Morrow and Company, Inc., 1987.

Graham, Billy. *The Collected Works of Billy Graham.* Nashville: Word Publishing, a division of Thomas Nelson, Inc., 1993.

Hannaford, Peter. *Ronald Reagan and His Ranch.* Bennington, Vermont: Images from the Past, 2002.

Hymns for the Family of God. Nashville: Paragon Associates, Inc., 1976.

John Hinckley, Jr. Trial: Transcript. 1982.

Linder, Doug. "The Trial of John Hinckley, Jr." University of Missouri-Kansas City, 2001.

Mapes, Creston. "Dream Dreams, Set Goals." *In Touch.* September 2003, Vol. 26, No. 9.

Meese, Edwin, III. *With Reagan: The Inside Story.* Washington, D.C.: Regnery Publishing, 1992.

Morris, Edmund. *Dutch: A Memoir of Ronald Reagan:* New York: Random House, 1999.

Muir, William Ker Jr. *The Bully Pulpit*. San Francisco, California: Institute for Contemporary Studies, 1992.

Noonan, Peggy. *When Character Was King*. Harmondsworth, Middlesex, England: Penguin Books, 2001.

Packer, J.I. *Knowing God*. Downers Grove, Illinois: InterVarsity Press, 1973.

Reagan, Maureen. *First Father, First Daughter*. Boston, Massachusetts: Little, Brown, and Company, 1989.

Reagan, Michael. *On the Outside Looking In*. New York: Kensington Publishing Corp., 1988.

Reagan, Nancy. *I Love You, Ronnie*. New York: Random House, 2000.

Reagan, Nancy. *My Turn: The Memoirs of Nancy Reagan*. New York: Random House, 1989.

Reagan, Ronald. *Abortion and the Conscience of the Nation*. Sacramento: New Regency Publishing, 2000.

Reagan, Ronald. *An American Life*. New York: Simon and Schuster, 1990.

Reagan, Ronald. "My Faith." *Modern Screen*. May 1950.

Reagan, Ronald, and Richard G. Hubler. *Ronald Reagan's Own Story: Where's the Rest of Me?* New York: Karz-Segil Publishers, 1965.

Reisser, Paul C.; editors, Vinita Hampton Wright, Lisa A. Jackson. *Parents' Guide to Teen Health*. Wheaton, Illinois: Tyndale House Publishers, Inc., 1997

Robinson, Peter. *How Ronald Reagan Changed My Life*. New York: Regan Books, HarperCollins Publishers, Inc., 2003.

Roe, Earl O. *Dream Big: The Henrietta Mears Story*. Ventura, California: Gospel Light Publications, 1990.

Schweizer, Peter. *The Fall of the Berlin Wall*. Stanford, California: Hoover Institution Press, 2000.

Schweizer, Peter. *Reagan's War*. New York: Doubleday, 2002.

Sesno, Frank. Interview. Reagan Legacy. History Channel. 25 November 2002.

Shepherd, David R. *Ronald Reagan: In God I Trust*. Wheaton, Illinois: Tyndale House Publishers, Inc., 1984.

Skinner, Kiron K., Annelise Anderson, and Martin Anderson. *Reagan: A Life in Letters* New York: Free Press, 2003.

Sproul, R.C. *The Invisible Hand*. Dallas, Texas: Word Publishing, 1996.

Stanley, Charles. *Finding Peace*. Nashville: Thomas Nelson Publishers, 2003.

Thomsen, Paul. *Operation Rawhide*. Santee, California: Institute for Creation Research, 1997.

van der Linden, Frank. *The Real Reagan*. New York: William Morrow and Company, 1981.

von Damm, Helene. *Sincerely, Ronald Reagan*. Ottawa, Illinois: Green Hill Publishers, Inc., 1976.

BIBLIOGRAPHY

Warren, Spencer. "Rediscovering the Classic Western." *American Outlook*. Summer 2003: Vol. VI, No. 3.

Wright, Harold Bell. *That Printer of Udell's*. Pelican Publishing Co., 1996

Yancey, Philip. *What's So Amazing About Grace?* Grand Rapids, Michigan: Zondervan Publishing House, 1997.

INDEX